# No More Bricks!
## Successful Whole Grain Bread
## Made Quick & Easy

Four Master Recipes With Over 30 Simple Variations
for a Healthy, Whole Grain Lifestyle

## Lori Viets

Knead to Know Press

Cowgill, Missouri

www.breadclass.com

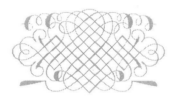

# Dedication

For David, Wyatt, & Weston

# Acknowledgments

First and foremost I owe a huge debt of gratitude to my husband and sons, who endured much and complained little during my roller coaster ride of first-time authorship. This project took so much more out of all of us than I ever could have imagined, and I couldn't have done it without their support. David took literally hundreds of photos, which is not an easy task when working with "live" dough under hot lights! He was also my "go to" guy for answers about all things mechanical, and offered valuable input with countless readings. Kathy Rude mentored me from the very beginning by introducing me to so many ways of healthier eating, freely sharing her wisdom and encouragement, and, along with her family, provided some unforgettable hands-on experiences for my family at Tree of Life Farm. The Crowther Family at Bread of Life Bakery sparked my "defining moment" by proving to me for the first time how truly good whole grain bread could be. Nanci Slagle at 30 Day Gourmet inspired me with her book and business model, both of which provided me with an opportunity to teach a very popular class and created a larger audience for my bread classes. Linda Drake became first my #1 fan, then my dear friend. She encouraged me with her success and is the only person I know who loves talking about bread and grains as much as I do. Bruce & Krista Wine offered lots of useful advice and support, and were invaluable for their help in getting the first edition of this book print-ready. Lynda Friend and Amanda Curtis provided the litmus test results that I needed to feel I was a "real" author after their early editorial readings. Mauricio Martinez not only coached me through the "labor pains" of writing, but he helped me realize how much I had to say and that I was a worthy enough person to say it. Finally, many thanks to all the students of my classes for sharing your triumphs, questions, ideas, and experiences, all of which continue to help me grow and learn.

# Disclaimer:

The purpose of this book is to educate and entertain. It is designed to provide information about the subject matter covered, and is sold with the understanding that neither the publisher nor the author is engaged in rendering medical advice or other professional services. If medical or other expert assistance is required, the services of a competent physician or health care provider should be sought.

This book is not intended to diagnose, treat, cure or prevent any disease. No one food or food group should be considered by itself to be either a prevention or a miracle cure for any type of physical ailment, disease, or disorder.

Every effort has been made to make this book as complete and as accurate as possible. However, there may be mistakes both typographical and in content. Therefore, this text should be used only as a general guide and not as the ultimate source of health information. It is not intended to reprint all the health information that is otherwise obtainable to individuals, but to complement, amplify, and supplement other texts.

The author and publisher shall have neither liability nor responsibility to any person or entity with respect to any loss or damage caused or alleged to be caused directly or indirectly by the information contained in this book.

If you do not wish to be bound by the above, you may return this book to the publisher for a full refund.

# Table of Contents

No More Bricks!

**Do you want to make bread RIGHT NOW?**

You can skip over the nitty-gritty details, if you promise to read them later, okay?

## 1. Assemble these ingredients:
- Hot Water
- Vegetable oil
- Sugar or Honey
- Whole wheat flour
- Salt
- Instant yeast
- Vital wheat gluten
- Dough Enhancer® (optional)
- Rolled oats (optional)
- Non-stick spray or oil

## 2. You will need this equipment:
- Mixer or machine of choice
- Measuring cups & spoons
- Loaf pans or baking sheets
- Instant-read thermometer
- Oven mitts
- Cooling rack

## 3. Choose a machine for specific directions:

## 4. Choose a master recipe to start with:

## 5. Read the following pages:

2

## My First Loaf

I grew up eating Wonder bread, or its generic equivalent, on a daily basis. On occasion my mother would dare to bring home a loaf of wheat bread, and I'm ashamed to say that I refused to eat it!

My first loaf of bread was made at the age of nine, when I went with my Girl Scout troop to a Bread Fair. As I saw the ingredients being passed out for Honey Wheat Bread-in-a-Bag, I was disappointed. The recipe used a mixture of about half white flour and half wheat flour, and I seriously considered hiding my wheat flour, so I wouldn't have to use it. It was called bread-in-a-bag, because we did all the mixing and kneading inside a plastic bag to contain the mess. It was fun to make, squishing all the ingredients together, but I expected that it would not taste very good at all. I was wrong...I thought that piping hot loaf of yeasty goodness was the best bread I had ever eaten! It probably was, since I'd had very few encounters with fresh home-made bread before.

I went home and made some more bread the next day. I felt proud to be able to make something so important, and I loved the aroma of just-baked bread all through the house. Despite its being "yucky" whole wheat, I even loved the taste of it. I was hooked, and I made the recipe over and over again. I still have that ragged, stained, flour-encrusted recipe card, from 25 years ago, and I show it reverently to the kids at the bread-in-a-bag classes that I now teach.

## The Brick Factory

Shortly after getting married, my husband and I became interested in improving our health in preparation for starting a family. At that point, I didn't really know much about the specific benefits of eating whole grains, I just knew it seemed more "natural." I decided to start making whole wheat bread, without the addition of any white flour. The thought of grinding fresh flour from actual wheat kernels never even crossed my mind. On the contrary, I thought that buying whole wheat flour off the supermarket shelf was very purist and self-sacrificing of me!

I confidently attempted my first super-healthy loaf; however, to my great surprise, I found that not only my trusty childhood recipe, but ANY recipe with which I tried using exclusively whole wheat flour, yielded a dense, dry brick. Despite having made bread for years, I thought that I must have done something wrong. I tried again and again, certain that a different recipe or more careful kneading would take care of the problem. Every time I followed the instructions to the letter, but the results were the same: dry, heavy bricks! Eventually I got tired of failure, so the frequency of my attempts grew farther and farther apart. By the time my two sons were born, I concluded that during this busy season of my life, I would have to give up the notion of making my own bread. I just didn't have time to waste making bread that no one, including me, wanted to eat. So I purchased 100% whole wheat sandwich bread from the store, determined that my kids would grow up accustomed to the taste and texture of whole wheat bread, whether they wanted to or not.

## My Kids Made Me Do It

Several years later, my boys and I were invited to go on a field trip with a group of students to tour an organic bakery that some friends of ours had just opened. They showed us how their whole grain bread was made, from the wheat which they milled into their own fresh flour, to the huge commercial mixer that mixed 40 quarts of dough, to the massive rotating oven that baked over 100 loaves of bread at once. We bought several different kinds of bread and some pizza crusts, and headed home. The drive from the bakery to our home took well over an hour, and I remember wishing we lived close enough to buy bread from this bakery all the time. The boys were complaining of being hungry, and rather than stop somewhere to eat fast food, I told them to open up some of the bread we had just bought. After the first few nibbles, they began exclaiming, "Mom! This is the best bread ever - you have to try some!" and "Can we buy this bread all the time?" and "This is WAY better than our bread at home!" They tore open all the other bags of bread, eager to try each kind, unable to decide which one was the best. One of the loaves was a multi-grain bread, loaded with crunchy seeds and cracked grains, that I assumed no one but me would eat. But there they were, both of them chowing down on even this loaf as if it were candy! My younger son shocked me to the toes by announcing that this "birdseed" one was his favorite. At that point I almost drove off the road - I couldn't believe it! My kids were actually enjoying – no, relishing – healthy bread, like I had never seen them do before. That did it! I decided that no matter what it took, I was going to find a way for us to have bread like this every day.

I did some quick mental calculations and immediately saw a problem. We already consumed, on average, about a loaf per day of store-bought bread at a price of $1-$2 per loaf, but I knew we'd probably eat much more of the good, premium stuff, at a cost of $4-$5 per loaf. Although it was well worth the price, it was not going to fit into our single-income budget, due to the fact that I'm at home full-time during the day to homeschool my kids. Once again, I'd have to resort to making my own bread, yet I dreaded the thought of one more difficult chore to add to my overcrowded day, another drain on my limited time and energy.

A few days later, I was sitting at my friend Kathy's kitchen table, while our children worked together on a school project. Her to-do list that day included making bread, and she told me that she'd like to send a loaf home with me for dinner. I looked doubtfully at the clock, thinking that I didn't have time to stay another four or five hours until the bread would be ready, but I watched as she poured wheat into her grain mill and assembled the other ingredients. I was already vaguely aware that she made all her family's daily bread, but she had mentioned more than once that she only liked to eat it when it was fresh from the oven. I thought that was "code" for "it doesn't taste very good any other way." I also just assumed she spent several hours each week on her baking. The next fifteen minutes proved my assumption wrong. I watched in amazement as she took six loaves' worth of bread dough out of her Bosch mixer and began shaping them into loaves and cinnamon rolls. I left her house about an hour later with a loaf of fresh, hot bread, that was ten times better than anything I'd ever made. I was also in complete awe of the existence of such a machine that could triple my previous output of two loaves of bread, requiring only a few minutes of time and virtually no effort on my part. The idea of grinding my own fresh flour began to blossom in my mind, too, and I was excited about my decision to return to breadmaking. Yet, I wasn't sure enough of my ability to justify the purchase of these expensive machines. I had bought "miracle" gadgets before, only to see them gather dust after the initial novelty of using them had worn off. Invariably, they ended up being sold at a garage sale for pennies on the dollar. I knew I needed to learn more in order to avoid repeating the bread failures of the past.

## A Surprising Truth

I began a serious quest to learn everything I could about bread and the grains to make it. I wanted to make not just good whole grain bread, but GREAT whole grain bread. I ordered every book and video I could find on the subject, hoping to discover any possible tip, no matter how obscure, that could help me to succeed this time. I even drove several hundred miles, along with my friend Kathy, to attend a weekend conference in Nebraska on how to make bread and other whole grain foods. By this time, I had read enough to learn some alarming truths about the effects of too much white flour. The importance of eating whole grains became a conviction for me, not just a passing fancy. I felt that my family's health was in serious jeopardy, and I was desperate to figure out how to improve it.

At first, my task was completely overwhelming. There was so much conflicting information presented in so many different ways. I read about and watched videos of chefs and professional bakers who preached precise weighing of ingredients and strict adherence to culinary methodology. I read books by extreme environmentalists who grew wheat in their backyards and baked bread in homemade brick ovens. I watched amateur videos of grandmothers and other home cooks slapping ingredients together haphazardly with bright smiles and vastly different "rules" and recipes. I wondered why Person A could make bread with one set of rules, but Person B could entirely contradict him and still present an apparently successful loaf of bread.

I gathered all the bits and pieces of information I had gleaned, and set to work. Being of a perfectionist mindset, I fretted over which was the "right" recipe to use, so I tried lots of them. Even though I didn't have all the answers yet (and still don't!), I was able to make the best bread I had ever made up to that point. With practice, more searching, and lots of trial and error, I began to improve. I still had little problems that I couldn't explain, but gradually I was able to fix most of them and understand why they had happened. Each batch got a little better than the one before. The more I experimented, the more those confusing terms and methods began to sink in. I finally realized that there was not one "right" way to make bread; there were many. Once a few key concepts were mastered, there were lots of choices. Baking bread could be just as simple or as complicated as I wanted it to be! What freedom! This was not at all what I had expected.

## Whole Grain Lifestyle

Becoming proficient at making bread completely transformed my whole approach to cooking and menu planning. In some ways, it made things easier. Meals became much simpler and more enjoyable. We loved the bread so much that we couldn't get enough of it and happily joked about being on a "bread and water" diet.

With new benefits came new challenges too. I had to make room in my kitchen for a grain mill, mixer, and more pans. I had to drive over an hour away to the nearest location where a semi truck would deliver bags of grain to members of our food co-op. Then those bags had to be hauled home and properly stored. It took some effort to figure out and set up a system, but it was worth it.

The phrase "whole grain lifestyle" stuck in my mind at some point, because it's not just a different way of eating. It often requires stepping outside of the typical American food distribution system. According to the Whole Grains Council website (wholegrainscouncil.org), "...the average American eats less than one daily serving of whole grains, and over 40% of Americans never eat whole grains at all." Yikes! That explains why it's hard to find basic whole grains at the local grocery store. After all, manufacturers and retailers will only make available what the majority of their customers will buy.

Because of the limited availability of ready-to-eat 100% whole grain foods, it's up to you fill in the gap, and that means a commitment to putting it all into practice. Don't get me wrong; it is feasible for anyone to do, and I hope this book will help make it easier for you. But you must expect to invest a little time and money up front in order to provide the best nutrition for your family.

In daily application, my interpretation of a whole grain lifestyle is to consume whole grains in at least one form, and preferably two at every meal. How else can you get that recommended daily intake of 6-11 servings? For me, one of the easiest ways is to use a variety of whole grain flours to replace white flour in as many recipes as possible.

In my opinion, grain, and especially bread, IS the staff of life, so it makes sense to me that it should be the foundation of a healthy diet. I try to build most of my family's meals around bread, making it the focal point, instead of just a filler. This led to the development of a few master recipes that are versatile enough to use for all of kinds of bread-based meals and snacks, such as soup bowls, pizza crusts, and sweet rolls.

By consuming more bread at each meal, the amount of other higher-calorie foods we eat is reduced, because the bread is so filling. This benefit is two-fold: physical and financial.

First, we all have begun to feel better in general and have more energy. The number of colds and other minor illnesses in our household seems to have decreased, reducing expensive medicines and doctor visits. The desire for between-meal snacks has also diminished, since eating more complex carbohydrates helps to keep blood sugar regulated. In the midst of the low-carb, anti-bread craze that swept America, I lost over 25 pounds, and have managed to keep it off, while eating all the bread I want!

Second, I can see a decrease in our grocery bill, because whole grains are one of the least expensive food groups. A loaf of homemade bread costs no more than $1, at the very most, and can be much less, if you purchase ingredients in bulk.

Now, having said all that, don't get the impression that I refuse to make allowances for eating any white flour, ever. On the contrary, my family still eats puffy, white dinner rolls at restaurants and decadent white cake at weddings and birthday parties. These are not daily occurrences, so I don't worry about them. Even at home, I find myself needing to buy the occasional package of hamburger buns, because there are just days when things don't go according to plan. I'm not perfect, and you don't have to be either.

I don't believe in being in bondage to "food theology," to the point of not being able to eat out or socialize in other people's homes. If you were to invite me to your home for a meal, I wouldn't want you to fret about what you served me. I'd just be glad for the chance to get to know you, and I think food should always be secondary to that.

## Me, An Author?

I never imagined that those early bricks I made would one day lead to writing my own recipes, much less a book!

It began by my teaching a basic bread class through a community education program. I really enjoyed teaching it, and the response was good. Gradually, I expanded by teaching at additional locations in surrounding suburbs, and by adding follow-up classes to show more advanced techniques. Soon requests for classes and presentations started coming in from church groups, companies, and local convention organizers, and I had more classes booked than I could keep up with. I spent a lot of time answering the same questions over and over, until I finally decided to put my knowledge into written form. So voilà, here it is!

My goal is to give you the kind of resource I longed for myself, but couldn't find, when I was learning to make bread. I've tried to condense all the best tips and tricks into a simple, user-friendly package that is neither tedious nor overwhelming, but inspires you to start baking right away, and to have quick success.

Bread is very personal, and it should reflect your unique tastes and preferences. Use my recipes as a starting point, and feel free to play around with them after a while. You may wish to use less sweetener or oil than I do. Or, you might prefer to slow down the rising process by adding additional time, or speed it up by using a bit more yeast. Keep a small notebook and record your experiments. Ask your family to rate the taste of each new loaf you create. Once you have discovered a combination that you really like, make it official by naming your bread and begin your own collection of custom recipes. I have even included a blank recipe form for you to do just that.

I'm still constantly tweaking my own recipes, because there is always more to learn, and more room for improvement. I hope that you'll enjoy the process as much as I do, and that you and your family will reap many rewards from a healthy, whole grain lifestyle.

No More Bricks!

# PART ONE

# BREAD CLASS

No More Bricks!

What Makes Bread So Hard?

Making Whole Grain vs. White Bread

Three Methods Compared

No More Bricks!

## What Makes Bread So Hard?

More than any other single food, the making of any kind of bread seems to overwhelm and mystify even the most competent of cooks. The reason for this became quite clear as I delved into my research of how to make great whole grain bread. Unlike almost any other recipe, there are countless variables contributing to its outcome. Take a cookie recipe, for example. Even though there are thousands of different cookies in the world, there is little variance in the way of mixing the ingredients together. It's very straight forward and direct. By following the recipe exactly, you could only ruin cookies by making major mistakes in measuring or by burning them. Not so with bread! Even the most careful baker can end up with terrible bread, without a clue as to what she did wrong. I've pondered over the reason for this and have come to the conclusion that there are three elements of breadmaking that cause both the recipes and the results to vary so widely.

Bread is

- one part method

- one part food science

- one part art

The method you choose is the first key, and that will be decided by the amount of time you want to spend and the sensitivity of your palate. Relatively speaking, the longer the process, the better the outcome will be. Think of a crusty loaf of artisan bread, a French baguette, for example. It has a unique texture and flavor that is unlike any other bread. It requires the effort of days, or sometimes even years, in the case of a starter dough that has been handed down from generation to generation. Compare that to a loaf from your bread machine. Still good, but no comparison really! The trade-off is time and convenience.

The food science aspect of bread is, truthfully, quite complex, what with all the invisible action of enzymes and bacteria. However, the understanding of a few basic rules that apply to all breadmaking will help you to manipulate most outcomes in your favor. There are also a few lesser-known tricks I uncovered that will help you improve your breadmaking skills immediately, but that means you have to be willing to un-learn a few "rules" that you thought were true.

The last element is art, or call it personal expression, if you don't feel you are an artist. But you are, because everyone is, or can be. Bread, like all cooking, is a form of art. That's one reason why it's known in so many forms all over the world, from Russian black bread to baguettes to San Francisco sourdough. I'm not saying you have to invent something brand new. Even if you follow my recipes and techniques to the letter, and don't change a thing, your bread will still be a little different from mine, because you are a unique individual. Some of your personal expression will be unconscious, like the way you hold your hands to shape your loaves. Your conscious creative contribution can be as simple as kneading in a handful of your favorite nuts or dried fruits to a standard bread dough recipe. I'll give you lots of ideas to get started, and then you can discover the artist within you that you never knew was there!

## Making Whole Grain vs. White Bread

Having broken down the components of breadmaking in general, it's important to point out that there are some major differences between making whole grain bread and white bread. Here are a few reasons why using 100% whole grain flour adds a new dimension of difficulty:

- Weight

- Texture
- Absorption
- Flavor
- Weight

The flour is heavier, because the extra bran and germ add weight, which means the yeast has a heavier load to raise. Using a little extra yeast or allowing extra rising time, as well as determining the right flour-to-liquid ratio, will help to compensate for this.

## Texture

Again, the "culprits" are bran and germ (those poor, misunderstood friends!). Unlike the uniform texture of powdery white flour, whole grain flour has tiny bits and pieces of bran and germ, which have sharp edges and rough texture. These can cut into the dough and damage the gluten strands, reducing the bread's ability to hold its rise.

## Absorption

It takes longer for whole grain flour to fully hydrate, or absorb liquid. This often causes bakers to add too much flour too fast, resulting in dry, dense loaves. This can be tricky for bakers bent on speed, like me. A little patience and an easy hand with the flour during mixing are key.

## Flavor

Whole grain flour has a tendency to mask the flavor of other ingredients. Not necessarily in a bad way, because the taste of freshly-ground flour is excellent, as opposed to commercially-ground flour. But you'll need to add more cinnamon to your cinnamon bread, and more herbs to your Italian bread to keep those seasonings from being "lost."

Breadmaking books and recipes typically fall into one of two categories: artisan or traditional. While less common, some recipes offer a "rapid" variation, and some bread machines have a speedy baking cycle, so a third option could be called express breadmaking.

## Artisan Breadmaking

Artisan bakers are highly-skilled craftsmen comparable to any fine artist. They are well-versed in the exacting food science of chemical reactions and use only the most basic ingredients of flour, water, salt, and yeast (often wild yeast captured from the air). For flavored breads, the additions would include only the highest quality and recognizable-as-food ingredients, such as butter, eggs, or herbs. They wouldn't think of using any chemical preservatives or dough conditioners, so the bread itself has an extremely short shelf life, only a few hours to one day at best. Artisan breads are made in small batches, shaped meticulously by hand, and baked at very high temperatures, often in hearth ovens. They are known for a specific texture and crust, delicate complexity of flavors, and an "old world" look, all brought about by multiple, long rising times in a tightly-controlled environment.

While it is possible to make an approximate version of an artisan bread at home, it is highly impractical to do on a regular basis for "everyday" bread. In addition, most artisan bread recipes are not made exclusively from whole grain flour, if indeed any at all. Some rely on patented specialty flours that are not commonly available in regular grocery stores.

## Traditional Breadmaking

This is the method most standard cookbooks teach. There are two ways of making bread by this method: the sponge method and the straight dough method (also called direct method). Either can be done by hand or with the aid of a machine.

Similar to artisan bread, the sponge method involves an extra step of making a batter (sometimes called pre-ferment or pre-dough) with a small amount of water, flour, active dry yeast, and sometimes sugar or honey. It will ferment anywhere from 30 minutes to several hours before being combined with the remaining dough ingredients. This initial slow fermentation helps to develop more flavor in the final bread. After kneading, the dough will rise a minimum of two times, up to three times (once or twice after kneading and once after shaping), before being baked.

The straight dough method is now the more commonly used one in modern cookbooks. The active dry yeast will be dissolved and proofed in warm water, then, just like it sounds, the dough ingredients are mixed together all at once and allowed to rise a total of two to three times before baking.

This is certainly a much more practical method, but depending on your schedule or the size of your family, may still be too time-consuming to keep up with your daily bread needs. Truth be told, most of the extra time involved is not hands-on work, but will still require you to oversee it for several hours. A traditional recipe will usually yield 1 to 2 loaves.

## Express Breadmaking

Now for the technique I advocate in this book, which I call the No More Bricks Quick & Easy method. No, I didn't exactly invent a new way to make bread. I've simply put together a combination of techniques and equipment usage that speeds up the process. It's really more of a mindset than anything: the idea that you can

make all of your family's bread plus lots of meal ideas from a bulk batch of bread dough.

This method is perfect for the beginning baker, because it's, well, quick and easy! I hesitate to call it foolproof, because there are still many little variables that can make a first loaf less than perfect. I'd prefer to call it a very user-friendly method.

In a nutshell, here' are the main points that make it different from the other methods:

- freshly milled flour

- master recipe + variations

- instant yeast

- spiral mixer (bulk batches)

- single rise

- freezer pantry system

It starts with milling fresh flour for maximum taste and nutrition. (This is part of what makes the bread successful - it's healthy, but it also tastes good at the same time!) A master recipe with shaping and flavor variations helps you quickly create all the different forms of bread your family needs and wants, plus lots of meal ideas. Then, using instant yeast and a spiral mixer, a bulk batch of up to six loaves is made, with the ingredients being mixed all at once and kneaded in just minutes. Next, the dough will be immediately shaped and given just one rise before baking. Finally, the extra is put into the freezer for later use. The whole process takes just about 75-90 minutes maximum, from start to finish.

You need to be aware, however, that there are a couple of potential drawbacks to this method. I say "potential," because personally, I don't think they are cause for serious concern. First, the flavor and texture of bread made this quickly will be different from that of bread that has been allowed more time to ripen and develop. This is the part I mentioned earlier about the sensitivity of your palate coming into play. Second, there is some controversy surrounding the presence of phytic acid in grains and its effects on nutrient absorption. It has been suggested by some that the bioavailability of certain minerals in grain is increased by prolonged fermenting and rising times, allowing them to be "unlocked" as they are broken down by enzyme activity. Based on evidence I have read, I don't subscribe to this belief. One thing is certain: you only have to eat one serving of bread to realize its obvious benefits of fiber, and that's something that can't be inhibited. However, if you feel it necessary, it's perfectly fine to allow for double or even triple rising with the recipes in this book. Of course, that will lengthen the overall process.

As I see it, it's better to make bread quick and have it available to eat on a daily basis, than to never get around to making any at all, because it takes too long. Besides, homemade bread will always be better in taste and nutrition than store-bought can ever be. I have yet to see those attending my bread classes do anything other than roll their eyes in absolute pleasure while savoring the miracle that is fresh-baked bread.

| Breadmaking Method | Artisan | Traditional Cookbook | No More Bricks Quick & Easy |
|---|---|---|---|
| Yield in Loaves | 1-2 | 1-2 | Up to 6 |
| 100% Whole Grain | Varies | No | Yes |
| Number of Risings | 2-3 | 2-3 | 1 |
| Approximate Time | 2-3 days+ | 4-6 hours | 75-90 minutes |

## Putting Thoughts into Action......

Why do you want to make bread? The more reasons you can identify, the more motivated you'll be to follow through. Check all that apply:

_____ I love bread!

_____ I need to save on groceries

_____ I need more fiber

_____ I enjoy baking

_____ I want to sell bread for profit

_____ I need simple meal ideas

_____ I want to share w/ friends/family

_____ I have dietary concerns

_____ Other: _____

_____ Other: _____

What Makes a Grain "Whole?"

Attention All White-Bread-Eaters!

The Case for Grinding Your Own Fresh Flour

Base Flours Vs. Blending Flours

Buying and Storing

No More Bricks!

## What Makes a Grain "Whole?"

A whole grain is the entire seed of a cereal plant, containing bran, germ, and endosperm. To say something is "whole grain" means that it's consumed in its whole, intact state, or is cracked, rolled, or ground, without any of its three component parts removed.

Most grains share the same basic structure, so to make things easy, I'll use wheat as my example. A grain of wheat is pretty small, and to most people, fairly unfamiliar, in terms of its makeup. To better illustrate its anatomy, which is paramount to your understanding of making bread, I like to compare its structure and physiology with something much more familiar: an egg. It's not a perfect analogy, but once you see it, I don't think you'll ever forget it or be confused by it again.

As you know, an egg has three parts: the shell, yolk, and white. These parts directly correlate to the three parts of a wheat berry (kernel), which are the bran, germ, and endosperm. Now, let's add just one more "body" part to each item: the egg carton that the eggs are sold in, and the husk that encases each grain. So far, our comparison looks like this:

- Egg carton = Husk
- Egg shell = Bran
- Egg yolk = Germ
- Egg white = Endosperm

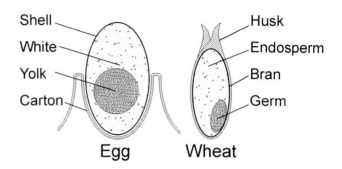

Keep this in mind as we talk about the function of each part of the grain.

The husk, sometimes called a hull, is simply packaging, like the egg carton. It holds the grain in place on the stalk, but is discarded after harvest. It's a paper-like substance that blows away in the wind, called chaff. I mention this part for two reasons. When shopping for grains, some types will be labeled as hulled, and I want you to know what it means. Anytime you see that, it's okay, because hulls are the inedible part. Second, when you get your grain home, there will sometimes be kernels in it that are still encased in their husks, or have pieces of husks interspersed. Just pull those out and discard them.

Next comes the bran, which is the equivalent of the eggshell. Well, almost. Here's where the analogy isn't 100% accurate, because you definitely want to consume the bran, but you don't eat eggshells (unless you're a very bad cook). But look at the function of the shell. It holds the egg intact, protecting the interior. That's what the bran does too. It's made up of several thin layers, similar to your skin, and serves to protect the wheat, holding all of the nutrition intact until it's broken open by milling or sprouting. You would never buy eggs that are cracked, right? In fact, you probably open the carton to make sure they're all intact. Similarly, you should avoid buying any grain that has been previously cracked or ground into flour. I'll explain why a little later.

Moving on to the germ. This, like the yolk, is the embryo, the new life contained within. The germ will sprout and grow into a wheat stalk, just like the yolk will grow and hatch into a chicken. Easy.

What sustains that life until it either hatches or sprouts? There's a built-in food supply, of course. The egg white, like the endosperm, is the source of food during initial growth, and it's made up mostly of carbohydrates and protein. Both the developing chick and the plant embryo will consume this starchy interior for food, until they can get their own food outside of their shells. The endosperm is the "powdered gold" of the milling industry, the part that is painstakingly separated from the bran and germ to produce refined white flour.

Here's another way to compare egg whites and endosperm. Have you ever made meringue for a pie? You separate the yolks out carefully, because even a drop of yolk will spoil meringue. Then you beat the whites vigorously, incorporating lots of air until they're tall and fluffy. Now, imagine that lily-white, spongy stuff for just a minute, and compare that to what is made from endosperm, after all the bran and germ are removed. Something tall, white, and fluffy with empty calories. Are you thinking Wonder bread?

Now that the parts of the grain are a little more familiar to you, let's talk about how they benefit your body. Since each grain has its own specific profile of nutrients, it's important to include a wide variety of them in your diet. We'll look specifically at the nutrients in the wheat berry.

## Wheat Bran

The bran contains some vitamins and several essential and trace minerals including iron, magnesium, phosphorus and calcium. Its primary benefit, though, is insoluble fiber, or "roughage." This is the indigestible, bulky material that acts like a slightly abrasive sponge. It absorbs water to many times its original size and pushes wastes out of the body, scrubbing the walls of the digestive tract clean in the process. Fiber helps you feel full, so you eat less, and it also promotes speedy removal of toxins from your body, which would otherwise spend too long in your digestive track, where they could be reabsorbed, causing potential disease.

Nutritionists do not agree on what the recommended daily intake of fiber should be. The range is anywhere from 25-40 grams per day, depending on who you ask, your age, and gender. Assuming you only need the lower amount, most people don't come close to getting enough, because the average American consumes less than 10 grams per day. This vital deficiency of fiber is linked to many of the diseases and ailments that plague us, which, coincidentally, are often unheard of in less affluent countries where whole grains are eaten regularly and there is little or no availability of refined foods.

## Wheat Germ

In addition to containing fiber and minerals as bran does, the germ is a concentrated powerhouse of many other nutrients, such as complex carbohydrates, protein, and essential fatty acids. It's an excellent source of B vitamins which are vital to the functions of metabolism, maintaining healthy skin and muscle, immune and nervous system function, and cell growth (especially in pregnancy). The wheat germ oil is a primary source of vitamin E, an important antioxidant, which is shown to have a role in preventing some forms of cancer and heart disease, among other benefits. It's this rich oil which makes flour so prone to spoilage, if not handled properly.

## Wheat Endosperm

The endosperm is mostly made up of carbohydrates, a main source of energy for the body. When eaten with the rest of the grain, it forms a complex carbohydrate which is burned slowly by the body, regulating blood sugar and energy levels. However, when stripped away from its bran and germ cohabitants, it becomes a simple carbohydrate, also known as "empty calories." Also contained in the endosperm of wheat are unique proteins, not found in most other grains, that combine with liquid (and some movin' & groovin' in the form of kneading) to create something you'll be hearing a lot about from now on: gluten.

## Attention All White-Bread-Eaters! (and the People Who Love Them)

So maybe you or your family are less than thrilled with the prospect of giving up your beloved white flour. I can relate, because I was once in your shoes. Learning two things helped me make the transition from "white" to "brown" with a little more ease. The first was finding out how white flour is made and the detrimental effects it can have on the body. The second was discovering that whole grains, when freshly ground and properly prepared, can actually taste better than their all-white impostors! In the hope that it will benefit you as well, I'll be sharing some disturbing facts about white flour, and then later we'll dive into the rainbow of tastes and textures that can be found in whole grain flours.

For those of you who are already whole grain "veterans," revisiting some of this information

should encourage you to keep fighting the good fight. Personally, I find that I need to be reminded frequently of things I already know. Each time I read or reread about the problems and diseases that are linked to the consumption of dead, white flour, I'm convicted all over again and inspired to work harder than ever to improve my family's diet. Even the choir needs to hear a good rousing sermon now and then!

## The Life and Times of White Flour

A fair percentage of those who attend my bread classes have absolutely no idea that white flour is not made from the whole grain. Words like bran and germ are only vaguely familiar to them. Many think that wheat vs. white flour is just a matter of bleaching. I've even been asked by eager students, "What do you buy to make flour ? I don't know what to look for at the store."

It's no wonder really, since white flour has been a pantry staple for many decades now. Most of us have never used anything else and our society, in general, has little contact with farms or agriculture. We use neutral words like "pork" and "beef" so we don't have to think about the fact that we're eating what was formerly a living, squealing pig or a peacefully grazing cow. Paradoxically, for a country that was originally settled largely due to its rich farmland, we place surprisingly little emphasis on where our food comes from. How did we get to this point of chemically industrialized food? What about those "amber waves of grain" we sing so proudly of?

Lest you think white flour is strictly an invention of modern Americans, call to mind the phrase "there's nothing new under the sun." To understand how we became dependent on nutritionally-devoid white flour, we'll have to take a whirlwind tour through the history of flour milling and breadmaking. We'll only make a couple of brief stops in the Old World, so we'll have more time to look at America's downhill slide into acceptance of the White Flour Lie. Ready? Here we go!

In his book, *Six Thousand Years of Bread: Its Holy and Unholy History*, author E.H. Jacob depicts images of Egyptian murals, some of the earliest recorded accounts of breadmaking. On them, lines of bald, skirted Egyptians dance their way through the entire baking process. There are farmers sprinkling seeds and cutting wheat (back then it was wheat's ancestor, emmer), laborers grinding and sifting, sifting and grinding. Apparently, they figured out that all this separating and regrinding of the grain would make artistic bread The end of the line portrays shelves and trays full of a myriad of tall, elaborately-designed loaves of bread fit for a king, er, I mean pharaoh.

The Greeks and Romans knew what the Egyptians did: grain sifted multiple times to remove the bran and germ made lighter bread. However, the difficulty arose from the intensive manual labor to produce it, making it more expensive. Thus, the color of one's bread became a status symbol which separated the noble rich from the poor and working classes. The historian Pliny recorded that bakers secretly mixed chalk with the flour, both to make it appear whiter and to make it stretch farther, thereby increasing their profits.

We could spend some time talking about bread in Europe in the Middle Ages, but instead let's fast forward, w-a-a-ay forward.

In our own nation's history, back before the Industrial Revolution of the late 1700's, most people still lived on or near the family farm. At the core of every community was a mill. When the farmer needed flour, he brought a sack of grain to the miller who milled it in exchange for some that he would keep for himself, the "miller's toll."

The extra flour or grain would be traded to local townspeople in exchange for other goods.

As our country continued to grow, factories sprung up, and more people moved away from the farm, seeking a better, easier life in the city. Larger mills had to be built to keep up with the demand of shipping flour to the crowded cities. But there was a problem. By the time the flour got to its destination, it would be spoiled, and the mills didn't want to lose money on flour that couldn't be sold. So they separated the flour, removing the bran and germ, ensuring that the flour would last not only through the long trip to the consumer, but could actually be stored in surplus. The by-products of bran and germ were sold for animal feed and pharmaceutical products, and became a source of great profit in and of themselves.

Like so many before them, American bakers also began to get sneaky by adding alum or chlorine to the slightly yellowish flour to make it even whiter. The people loved their "boughten" white bread; it gave them a sense of prestige and position. They spurned the rough, homemade, country bread that was a symbol of poverty. Does this sound familiar?

Much to the outrage of millers and bakers alike, there were a few radicals who wanted to rain on the parade of white flour "progress." Sylvester Graham was one such rebel who dared to suggest that people were sacrificing their health by eating white bread loaded with unsafe chemical additives. In 1829, he began making his version of Graham flour, which was coarsely-ground whole grain flour. He used this to make bread and (did you guess?) the famous Graham cracker, a "digestive biscuit" which, unfortunately, bears no resemblance whatsoever to our present-day version, made with refined white flour and corn syrup. While graham flour is commonly available for purchase in stores today, it's most often a counterfeit made of an inferior grade of flour mixed with a little bran. While containing slightly more fiber, it's decidedly not the pure, unbolted flour that its namesake intended it to be.

## Fast forward about 50 years.

Despite the effort of the "Grahamites," public demand for white flour continued to rise. Up to this time, many inventions had been introduced in the milling industry to improve output and working conditions, but one invention rendered all the mills before it obsolete. In 1882, Minnesota Governor John Pillsbury (think Pillsbury Doughboy) and his nephew Charles opened the largest mill ever built in America up to that time. They had toured mills all over Europe and brought back the newest steel roller mills, which produced white flour more efficiently than ever before. It was produced by the thousands of barrels per day, and later exported to England and beyond.

## A short leap of a couple decades...

Beginning in 1907 and throughout the 1920's and 1930's, the diseases of pellagra and beriberi became inexplicably common. Both diseases are caused by a vitamin B-complex deficiency, but because nutritional science was a very new field at that time, the existence of vitamins and minerals and their role in the functions of the body was just being discovered. Finally, in the late 1930's and early 1940's the link between vitamin deficiency and disease was proven, and millers were urged to stop removing the vitamin-rich bran and germ from flour. But they refused to give up their lucrative markets for both white flour and its by-products. They bargained with the government for a compromise whereby they would add a few synthetic nutrients back into the flour. In 1943, the government made the deal official by legislating the addition of three B-vitamins (thiamine, riboflavin, niacin) plus one mineral, iron, giving birth

to the term "enriched" flour. While some health officials argued that there were still many more shortcomings of white flour, the level of pellagra, beriberi, and another common problem, anemia, declined, and the public trusted that any further dietary deficiencies could and would be solved by government-mandated fortification of foods.

Despite the rapid advancement of nutritional knowledge in the decades following, no other vitamins or minerals were added for over fifty years. In 1998, another B-vitamin, folic acid, was found to be so vital to fetal development that it became the fifth supplement to white flour. While a few manufacturers of white bread voluntarily fortify some of their brands with calcium and other minerals, only the four B-vitamins mentioned plus iron are required by law. Just five nutrients, out of a known 30 nutrients contained in the wheat berry, are replaced. How could this be thought of as "enrichment?" Let's be honest and admit that it's a complete rip-off! We're also being led to believe that those five artificial nutrients are of the same quality and will be absorbed by the body in the same manner as naturally-occurring ones, when, in fact, that's not the case. Test tube supplements are never any match for Mother Nature; if they were, Americans would be among the healthiest people on the planet.

If the lack of vitamins, minerals, and phytochemicals was the only problem associated with white flour, it would be enough. Unfortunately, what's been taken away is only half the issue; what remains to be examined is the plethora of non-nutrient chemical treatments that are loaded into the bargain.

According to a list of FDA-approved food additives, known as the Federal Register (fda.gov – search for "food additives status list"), there are 93 chemicals that can or have been used in the past to "improve" flour and bread. Here's a partial listing: benzoyl peroxide, potassium alum, calcium sulfate, aluminum sulfate, calcium carbonate (chalk) acetone peroxide, ammonium phosphate, ammonium chloride, calcium bromate, calcium peroxide, nitrogen peroxide, and a host of other "ates," and "ides." Because they are considered "standard," most of these do not even have to appear on the label!

The most controversial additives include bleaching and maturing agents. One bleaching agent, nitrogen trichloride, was banned by the FDA because of its harmful effects, but not until after it had been used for twenty-five years! Its replacement, chlorine dioxide, is reportedly even more potent. Potassium bromate is a maturing agent that artificially ages flour, which bakers feel improves its elasticity and rising ability. Its use has long been banned in Europe because of its link to causing cancer. It was banned by the United Kingdom in 1990, the World Health Organization in 1993, Canada in 1994, China in 2005, with more countries in Asia, Africa and South America following suit. In the U.S., only the state of California regulates that its use in any product must be declared on a warning label. While the FDA has urged bakers to voluntarily stop using potassium bromate, it remains on the FDA list classified as GRAS, or Generally Accepted as Safe, because under "proper conditions" it will be completely used up in the baking process. However, it's generally agreed that at least some residue remains.

### "Western" Diseases

Prior to World War II, the most prevalent diseases were infective ones, those related primarily to lack of hygiene, antibiotics, and safe food handling practices. Advances in medical science began to reduce the causes of these diseases through public education and the invention of antibiotics and vaccines. However, a new breed of non-infective diseases began to emerge, which were nearly unheard of in other less industrialized cultures.

This phenomenon of "Western" diseases was first documented by Irish-born Dr. Denis Burkitt, who compared the medical cases during his twenty years of practice among the poorest cultures in Africa with those of Britain and North America. His ground-breaking research concluded that diet, specifically the absence of dietary fiber (both soluble and insoluble), was a major contributing factor to the rising number of non-infective diseases, as well as other common ailments, such as:

- diverticulitis
- appendicitis
- diabetes
- heart disease
- colorectal cancer
- gallstones
- hiatal hernia
- constipation
- hemorrhoids
- varicose veins
- obesity

This is not to say that the eating of any one particular food is a magical prevention or cure-all for disease, but studies show that risk factors are reduced for those who eat a variety of fiber-rich foods, including whole grains, legumes, fruits, and vegetables.

One final thought: if your diet is currently lacking in fiber, please don't try to significantly increase your fiber intake all at once. You'll miss work tomorrow!

Here are just a few of the articles and booklets I recommend for further reading:

- "Nutritional Content of Whole Grains Vs. Their Refined Flours" (Walton Feed, waltonfeed.com)

- "Flour," Microsoft® Encarta® Online Encyclopedia 2007, http://encarta.msn.com © 1997-2007 Microsoft Corporation. All rights reserved.

No More Bricks!

- "Some Facts About Food Additives" (Guyer Institute of Molecular Medicine, guyerinstitute.com)
- "How to Greatly Reduce the Risk of Common Diseases" (Medical Training Institute of America, 1990)

## The Case for Grinding Your Own Fresh Flour

Okay, so hopefully you're now convinced to use 100% whole grains in your breadmaking. But are you still on the fence about this whole flour milling thing? Does it still seem like a lot of trouble when flour is readily available at stores everywhere? I understand, because for years, I purchased whole wheat flour at the health food store, thinking I was doing good and never dreaming that I wasn't getting all of the whole grain. Later, when I learned the truth, I was hopping mad! I couldn't believe how I'd been cheated out of better taste and nutrition my whole life.

The truth is, you can make bread from any kind of flour you buy. But you owe it to yourself to at least be informed of the benefits of fresh flour and to give yourself time to get used to the idea.

Why bother to mill fresh flour?

- Guaranteed 100% whole grain
- No risk of rancidity
- Maximum vitamin retention
- Taste, taste, taste!
- Easy to use a variety of grains
- Saves money on groceries
- Reduces calories

Wow, I'm making a lot of big claims here. Let's talk about each one a little more.

## The "Whole" Story

It's a little-known fact that so-called "whole wheat flour" does not always contain the entire wheat kernel, just as "whole wheat bread" does not. It can truthfully be labeled "whole wheat" because that's the grain the flour was derived from, as opposed to rye or oats. That does not mean that all of what was ground from the grain actually made it into the bag.

Modern flour milling is an incredibly complicated process involving miles of conveyor belts between countless rollers, sifters, and sizers. All of the grain coming into the mills that produce flour for the big-name companies is separated into its component parts. The flour from each variety of wheat must be tested for protein content and then blended with other varieties to meet standards for specific types of flour. This ensures that an all-purpose flour, for example, has a consistent amount of protein in every bag in every store. So most whole wheat flour is actually white flour that has had some of the bran and even less of the germ (if any at all ) added back into it - just enough that it gets enough color and texture to make it look wheaty, but not so much that it won't be able to endure months of sitting on the shelf. he resulting proportion of bran, germ, and endosperm in this "whole wheat" flour is not what it would have been if the parts hadn't been sifted and remixed.

In addition, most types of flour are treated with a chemical potpourri of various conditioners, preservatives, bleaching agents, maturing agents, and/or fungicides to further lengthen their shelf life. Milling your own flour is the only way to ensure that you're getting grain that has had nothing desirable taken away, nor anything undesirable added to it.

It should be noted that there are some mills that specialize in supplying health food stores and upscale grocery stores with a range of common and not-so-common whole grain flours. These mills actually do grind the flour just the way you would expect them to and package the final product. They are often clearly marked with cold storage instructions on them, but as you'll see in a moment, it's too little, too late, in my opinion.

## Vitamin Oxidation

As soon as grain is cracked open, its vitamins begin to oxidize, reacting with the oxygen in the air to undergo chemical changes. It's the same principle as with fresh fruit, like apples or bananas. They begin to turn brown very quickly as soon as they are cut or peeled and exposed to air. You can't see this happening in flour, but it does. In as little as 72 hours of milling, nearly all of the B-vitamins are lost, unless they are preserved by refrigeration or freezing.

## Rancidity

Another problem with storing whole grain flour is that the oil contained in the germ of the grain, like any other fresh, unprocessed oil, is highly perishable. It needs to be used or properly stored before it becomes rancid. Rancidity is the decaying of fats caused by – again – oxidation. Think of it as the oxygen in the air "digesting" the fats. When this happens inside your body, it's properly assimilated, but with no where to go, it sits there and putrefies. The fats literally begin to break down and spoil, like rotten meat. Free radicals are released in this process and cause foul odors. You can't see rancidity, but you can definitely taste it. Rancid flour tastes flat, stale, and then bitter. Since most people have never tasted fresh flour, they have no point of reference and logically conclude that the wheat itself has bad flavor. Other foods besides grains are prone to rancidity, too. Take nuts, for example. You've probably eaten pecans or walnuts at some time that had a very bitter taste. That's because they were old, and the oil in them had become rancid.

Whole grains, protected intact inside their bran shell, have no exposure to oxygen. Once they are cracked or ground, they must be stored in a cool, dark place in an airtight container. This will not stop the oxidation process, but it does slow it down.

How long does it take to go rancid? The general consensus among manufacturers seems to indicate a shelf life of three months, but some sources suggest as little as seven days. That's only one week! Keep in mind, that shelf life is from the date of milling, NOT from the date of purchase. For myself, I play it safe and grind my flour right before I use it, and immediately store leftovers in the freezer.

The bottom line is, If you purchase commercially-ground whole grain flour from the store, it should be refrigerated all the way from the mill itself to the store display. If it isn't, and none that I know of are, don't buy it. You have no idea how long it's been sitting there, how long it spent in transit, or how long it sat in a warehouse. Notice that many of the labels on these packages of flour suggest storage in the fridge or freezer for optimum freshness. I find that hilarious. Isn't that a little like buying fresh milk that's been stored at room temperature, then taking it home and putting it in your fridge to keep it fresh? The damage has already been done, people.

## Whole Wheat Flour Is Easily Contaminated

Whole grain flour is very susceptible to bacterial invasion, especially if it's not kept in an airtight container and is left at room temperature. The rich nutrients in whole grain flour are a perfect place for airborne microorganisms to take up residence and reproduce, causing flour to mold and deteriorate very quickly. White flour takes much longer to grow moldy because there are not as many nutrients to "feed" the bacteria, and it's often been treated with fungicides to make it mold-resistant.

A few years ago, my son had a science assignment to observe molding bread. We decided to take the experiment one step further by comparing mold growth on homemade bread and store-bought bread. We deliberately encouraged mold growth by moistening the two pieces of bread, placing them in separate sandwich bags, and leaving them in the warm, moist environment of our water heater closet. We continued to spritz them with water every couple of days and recorded the changes. The homemade bread began to show signs of mold within 24 hours. Within two to three days, it was a kaleidoscope of greens and yellows, and within a week it had a thick growth of greenish-white "fur." Yet the store-bought bread was completely unaffected. We knew that it contained preservatives and chemicals that would make it more resistant to mold, but we didn't think it would be so completely unaffected under such conditions! We couldn't even make it grow mold on purpose. When something will not decay, you have to ask yourself if it was really alive to begin with.

## Fresh Flour Tastes Better

Who can resist the smell of freshly-ground coffee beans, or the extra zing of peppercorns ground right at the table? Unfortunately, most people have grown accustomed to the slightly bitter, stale flavor of store-bought whole wheat flour. It's no surprise that white bread is often preferred. It's not so much that it tastes better, it's just that it does not taste bad (because it has virtually NO flavor at all). Please believe me when I tell you that you have never really tasted wheat until you have eaten it freshly ground. It's not like anything you have had before. Without fail, at least one person in each of my bread classes declares, "This doesn't even taste like wheat!" That's because they are actually tast-

ing fresh wheat for the first time! I regularly get notes from my students about the successful bread they are baking for their friends and family. They report that everyone claims it's the best bread they've ever tasted. It's all because of the fresh flour and the simple techniques I'll share with you in this book.

## Variety

Owning a grain mill is the easiest way I know of to make sure you include a variety of grains in your diet. Most grain flours are interchangeable with wheat flour (make sure to use wheat as a base for your yeast bread though). The next time you bake muffins or mix up pancakes, instead of using wheat, try using flour from a different grain, such as barley or rye, or even a combination of grains. For convenience, I mill several kinds of flour at one time, in varying amounts. They will keep for two weeks in the fridge, or in the freezer for up to three months, with minimal loss of nutrients.

A variety of grains means a variety of nutrients. You would not think of eating carrots as your only source of vegetables all year long. You'd soon grow tired of them and perhaps even get an overdose of carotene, turning your skin yellow! If apples were the only fruit you ate, you'd dread the sight of them after a while, and dream of bananas and oranges. The same holds true with grains; you should not rely solely on one kind. Even though most grains look incredibly similar, each has its own unique taste and texture, just as fruits and vegetables do. It's easier to keep from getting bored when you have more choices. Each grain also has its own profile of vitamins, minerals, protein, and fiber, just as citrus fruits are famous for vitamin C, while bananas are known for their potassium content.

I think this intense focus on wheat, to the exclusion of almost all other grains, may be one possible explanation for the apparent rise in cases of persons who are allergic to wheat or have intolerance to gluten. It could be that the body just gets too much of this one grain, especially when it has been degenerated into lifeless white flour. Grains were meant to be consumed in their whole state. When you separate one component part from the rest, it leads to overconsumption of that part. Without the balancing effects of the rest of the grain, it's possible that the body simply cannot handle the higher concentrations of gluten and begins to reject it. Think of it this way. Have you ever eaten so much of one particular food that you literally made yourself sick? It seemed so good at the time that you just couldn't stop eating it, and then....uh-oh. Chances are, you've had an aversion to that particular food ever since. Your body is programmed with safeguards like this to help you choose to eat a balanced diet.

## Saving Money and Cutting Calories

When my first son was two years old, he especially loved to eat pancakes. Since he was significantly underweight for his age, due to complications during my pregnancy, we were thrilled to feed him anything he would eat. His grandparents would take him out to eat at pancake houses and local all-you-can-eat pancake breakfast fundraisers, where he would invariably gather a crowd of amused bystanders. It was a running joke in the family about how he could out-eat a lumberjack in pancakes. As he grew, he learned to like more kinds of foods, but pancakes remained a staple meal at our house. In those days, I used white flour in my recipes most of the time, because I hadn't yet learned about good-tasting fresh wheat flour. Each one of us could eat a stack of pancakes, sometimes along with eggs and/or sausage. We would eat our fill, but a couple of hours later, we'd all be hungry again. You know, like when you eat Chinese food.

Since I have switched to using 100% whole grain flour, we can barely finish two pancakes by themselves, let alone just one if we eat something else with it. That's because of the extra fiber in the bran and germ, which acts like a sponge placed in water. It swells up, giving you a full feeling. Not eating the extra pancakes, means not eating the extra butter and honey that would have gone on them. In addition, the complex carbohydrates burn more slowly, keeping blood sugar regulated, and eliminating the urge to snack between meals. To sum up, we get more nutrition from less food, save money by eating less food, and save calories by eating less food. Now that my sons are entering the teen years, it's good to know I'm prepared for the "bottomless pit syndrome." Oh, and one more thing. Now I can either make half the batch size I did before, or else have leftovers to freeze for another "free" meal. Either way that means a little less time that I had to stand over the stove. That's almost as good as saving money and calories!

Now I know this is may sound like an isolated example; not every meal can be pancakes. But regardless of what you serve, the same thing happens when you add a slice of bread, a dinner roll, or a bread bowl to your meal. You don't have room to eat as much of the other stuff as you normally would have.

Are you starting to see how adding fresh 100% whole grain flour to your diet can help you in more ways than you imagined? Great! Then skip the next section and move on to Base Vs. Blending Flours.

## If You Choose Not to Mill Your Own Flour

I realize there are some of good reasons why you may choose not to mill your own flour. You may feel the need to prove yourself in the ability to make bread at all, before diving in all the way with a grain mill. That's kind of how I felt at first, too. But hey, I didn't say you had to mill your own flour at home. Increasingly, there are do-it-yourself flour mills provided at some grocery stores and health food stores, just like the coffee grinders for fresh coffee. You will pay more for your grain, and often you'll be limited to only one or two types of grain and a single texture option. But it's a great way to try it out without any up-front equipment investment. Or, you may know someone who owns a mill that you can borrow. Sometimes small groups of friends who have attended my class will pool together and buy one mill to share. You don't have to have it every day; once a week or even once a month could suffice, depending on how much you want to bake or how much freezer space you have.

Do you feel it's just too far outside of your comfort zone to mill fresh flour? To some people it seems a little hoity-toity and Martha Stewart-ish. To others, it's like some weird Granola-tari-an thing. People often jokingly ask me if I grow my own wheat in my backyard, while surreptitiously looking at my feet to see if I'm wearing Birkenstock sandals. I will admit that home flour milling is not the mainstream thing to do, but Honey, it needs to be! When I was a kid, water came from the tap, and coffee came in a red can. Now, bottled water is "in," and you're just not serious about coffee if you don't grind your own beans. I hope that someday the same holds true for grinding fresh flour.

Whatever your reasons for not milling your own flour, please do consider it for some future time. Let it simmer in the back of your mind for a while. The important thing is to start making bread, and get more whole grains down your hatch. In the mean time, you want to know what the next best thing is, so I'll tell you.

If you do decide to buy flour, these are my suggestions, in order of best nutritional value:

Purchase freshly-ground flour from a friend or a retail store with a grain mill.

Look for whole grain flour that is kept refrigerated at health food stores. Choose a store that does a brisk business, so that the stock is kept rotated and fresh. Check to see if it's been dated for a clue as to how long it's been there.

Purchase a major brand of wheat flour (de-germinated and partially de-branned) from the grocery store, and store it in the refrigerator or freezer.

If you must use some white flour in your bread to help you get used to whole grain flour gradually, please purchase UNBLEACHED flour. As much as possible, try to avoid bleached white flour.

## Base Flours Vs. Blending Flours

When it comes to making yeast bread, not all flours are created equally. In fact, choosing the wrong flour is the surest way to end up with a brick. I think it will help you to think of flours as belonging to one of two groups - base flours and blending flours.

### Base Flours

There are only three grain flours that can be used on their own to make a soft, airy loaf of bread:

- wheat
- Kamut®
- spelt

Although any flour or combination of flours can be added to your bread recipe, a base of one of these three wheat-related grains is necessary to produce the familiar texture of a traditional American sandwich bread. The reason? They are the only ones with sufficient gluten (a specific type of protein we'll explore in depth later) to stand alone. Let's take a closer look at each one, then we'll explore a few other flours that you can experiment with later. Remember that any of these base flours or a combination of them can be used in any of the master recipes in this book with equal success.

## Wheat

The "King of Grains" is probably the most familiar of all the cereal grains. There are six main classes of wheat with over 30,000 varieties. Each class has characteristics that will produce different results in your baking.

- Hard Red Winter Wheat

- Hard Red Spring Wheat

- Hard White Wheat

- Soft White Wheat

- Soft Red Winter Wheat

- Durum Wheat

The terms "hard" and "soft" refer to the amount of protein in the wheat's endosperm. This is the most important distinction to make when purchasing your grain or flour.

Hard wheat can be used for any type of baking or cooking, but it's absolutely essential for using with yeast breads. It contains more protein than soft wheat. While it tends to produce heavy muffins and other baked goods, I use it all the time for pancakes and tortillas.

Soft wheat is not to be considered a base flour, but a blending flour. Often called "pastry wheat" it's ideal for any recipe that does not contain yeast, such as quick breads, cookies, and cakes. Read more about this flour in the Blending Flours section.

Winter wheat is sown in the fall and harvested in the summer. Because of a longer, drier grow-ing season, it contains slightly less protein than spring wheat.

Spring wheat does most of its growing during the wet spring months, which results in a slightly higher protein content than winter wheat. For this reason, it's generally the most preferred for breadmaking.

Red and white wheats each have unique tastes and produce slightly different loaves. Red wheat has a stronger "wheaty" flavor that is preferred by some purists who claim that white wheat has no flavor at all. It bakes into darker colored loaves that are a little smaller and denser than white wheat. I tend to prefer white wheat myself, and use it at all my baking classes. It makes a paler, fluffier loaf, and people are often amazed that it really is 100% whole wheat, because the taste is so mild. Still others prefer to mix the two wheats together in their bread recipe, to get the benefits of both flavor and lightness of texture.

Durum wheat is used almost exclusively for making pasta. Despite the fact that it has the highest protein content of all the wheats, its gluten-forming ability is not as suitable for breadmaking.

## Spelt

An ancient ancestor of modern-day wheat mentioned in the Old Testament, spelt is gaining in popularity because it has been found to be more tolerable by those who are allergic to wheat. While it has a lower gluten content than wheat, it is sufficient for bread making. Spelt can be substituted in any recipe calling for wheat, but will require a greater amount of it because of its fine texture, which is similar to that of soft wheat pastry flour. Spelt berries are a little larger compared to wheat berries, and have a pleasant, nutty flavor. Because it's more difficult to harvest, spelt is also more expensive than wheat.

## Kamut®

Kamut® (kuh-MOOT) is a trademarked name which is purported to mean "wheat" in Egyptian. It's an ancient relative of durum wheat, and is said to have been discovered in 1949 in an Egyptian tomb and brought to America for cultivation, giving it the nickname of "King Tut's Wheat." Like spelt, Kamut® is also favored by some who are allergic to wheat, and is becoming known as "the wheat you can eat." The berry is much larger and more elongated than wheat, like giant rice, making it easy to identify. When milled into flour, it has a beautiful golden color and bakes into a very tender, almost cake-like bread with a mildly sweet, buttery flavor. Because it is a licensed product, its distribution is strictly controlled, which shows up in the price per pound - up to three or four times the cost of common wheat.

## Grains for Blending Flours

Once you are comfortable making the master recipes in this book, there is no end to the variety of flavors and textures that can be achieved by mixing other grain flours into your bread. Remember, too, that each grain has varying quantities and qualities of specific nutrients – minerals, vitamins, soluble & insoluble fiber, proteins, carbohydrates, and phytochemicals – and that variety in all food groups is key to a healthy diet.

Any flour that is not hard wheat, spelt, or Kamut® is what I classify as a blending flour. In creating your new bread recipe, a good rule of thumb is to use a ratio of 75% base flour to 25% blending flour (unless otherwise noted for specific flours). Here are a few examples, using a one-loaf recipe (3 cups flour) for simplicity's sake:

2 ¼ cups of wheat flour

¾ cup cornmeal

**OR**

2 ¼ cups Kamut® flour

+ ¼ cup barley flour

+ ½ cup rolled oats

**OR**

2 ¼ cups spelt flour

+ ¼ cup millet flour

+ ¼ cup oat flour

+ ¼ cup rye flour

You'll be learning that it's actually better not to measure the flour exactly when making bread, but the above measurements will give you a good estimate of the ratios you should strive for.

Here's a brief look at some grains you can purchase to mill into flour at home. The nutrition notes listed here and throughout the book are not intended to be complete or in any way diagnostic, but are given in an effort to encourage experimentation with what may be unfamiliar uses for these grains.

**Amaranth** is not a true grain, but is actually an annual herb whose tiny seeds hail from Central America where they were once the sacred food of the Aztecs. Amaranth is often called a "Super Grain," because it contains essential amino acids not found in common grains. When combined with wheat, corn, or brown rice, it provides a complete protein, equal to red meat. It's easily digestible, and is higher in fiber, calcium, and iron than wheat. Because of its oil content, it's best stored in the refrigerator to avoid rancidity. Too small to mill on its own, mix amaranth with wheat or another larger grain before running it through your grainmill.

**Barley** is a confusing grain to try to buy. Look for hulled or hull-less, (remember the egg carton) but not pearled, pot, or scotch barley, which have all been "polished" to varying degrees to remove the bran and part of the germ. According to the National Barley Foods Council, barley may be one of our most underused grains in terms of food consumption. Only about 2% of barley grown is used in food products – the rest is for animal feed and malt production. It's rich in both soluble and insoluble fiber, vitamins, minerals, and phytochemiclas.

**Buckwheat** is not related to wheat at all; it's the pyramid-shaped seed of the buckwheat flower. A good source of protein, its dark flour is famous for pancakes. Roasted buckwheat is used to make the cereal kasha. Use buckwheat flour only in small amounts in your bread, due to its overpowering flavor.

**Corn** is a good source of iron, but is low in amino acids lysine & tryptophan, which is why it's often eaten with beans for complete protein. Commercially-ground cornmeal is almost always de-germinated, a significant loss because the size of the germ in corn is 11% of the total grain vs. 2% in wheat. Stone-ground whole cornmeal is very quick to turn rancid, so there's a pronounced difference in the taste of freshly-ground. Corn is one whole grain that's easy to find at your local grocery store – just buy plain popcorn kernels! It comes in a bag or jar, next to the microwave popcorn bags. Grind popcorn on your mill's lowest speed and coarsest texture setting. It makes amazing cornbread and adds great taste and texture to yeast breads, especially for spicy or cheesy breads.

**Millet** is a tiny, round, yellow seed that looks like birdseed, hence the name of my recipe "Crunchy Birdseed Bread." It has a nearly-complete range of amino acids, and can do anything rice can in recipes. For bread, grind

it into flour or add it whole and uncooked for a pleasant, crunchy texture.

**Oats** do wonders for lightening the texture of all breads and baked goods with a natural preserving quality that helps them stay fresh longer. They're high in protein, minerals, soluble fiber, and disease-fighting antioxidants.

Buying oats can be a little confusing, so here's a run-down of its forms:

**Oat groats** are the whole oat kernel that can be milled into flour in your grain mill. A special attachment for the Bosch Universal Plus mixer allows you to quickly roll your own oat groats (or other grains) for optimum freshness and nutrition. Some stand-alone manual units also roll or flake grains.

**Steel cut oats** are raw groats cut into 2 or 3 pieces, also called Irish, Scotch, or pinhead oats. Best for cereal, or use cooked leftovers for added flavor and texture in your bread.

**Regular rolled oats** are whole groats that have been steamed and rolled into flakes (each flake is one groat), then dried. Consider these as part of the flour in your recipes, and add them just as they are. If you want flour from rolled oats, buzz them in your blender or food processor, but NOT your grain mill, or it will clog.

**Quick Oats** are steel-cut oats that have been steamed and rolled into flakes, then dried. These highly-processed grains are smaller and thinner than regular rolled oats, so they cook more quickly.

**Quinoa** (KEEN-wah) the second of the two "Super Grains" is not really a true grain either, but a fruit. Like amaranth, it's growing in popularity because it's nearly a complete protein in and of itself. Traditionally grown by the Incas in the Andes Mountains, it was known as the "Mother Grain" because of the reputed longevity of those who ate it. Coated with its own natural pesticide, called saponin, it must be thoroughly rinsed or it will taste soapy. To avoid clogging your mill with wet grain, look for pre-washed quinoa for milling into flour.

**Rice** is "brown" even when its bran is colored red, purple, or black rice; all of these are forms of the whole grain. Rice has a thin layer of bran, giving it less fiber than other grains and making it the most prone to rancidity even in its whole unground state. Buy it in small quantities and use it within six months, or store it in the fridge or freezer. Brown rice flour has a nutty flavor and is similar to white flour in texture. It's often used to add crispiness to cookies and crumb coatings that will be fried.

**Rye** is rich in niacin and riboflavin, iron, cal-cium, phosphorus, and potassium. It also contains the most lysine of any of the grains. Because of its lower gluten content, rye flour is best combined with wheat flour at a rate of 25% rye to 75% wheat, up to a rate of 50% rye to 50% wheat, depending on the desired density of the bread.

The flavor of rye is actually quite mild; if you think you don't like rye bread, it's probably the flavor of the caraway seeds used in the recipe, not the rye, that offends you. Rye is a major component of the hearty traditional breads of Northern Europe because of its ability as a crop to withstand colder climates than wheat.

The characteristic greenish-gray kernels pro-duce a slightly darker flour than wheat, but most of its color "reputation" comes from the addition of other dark-colored ingredients in recipes where rye is typically featured. Along with a little flavor, the following can give rye bread the appearance of being dark brown to almost black: molasses, brewed or instant cof-fee granules, cocoa, or dark chocolate.

**Soft wheat** is one of the six classes of wheat. With its lower percentage of protein and higher moisture content, it should not be used alone for making yeast bread. However, it can be added to any base flour for softer, lighter bread, dinner rolls, and sweet rolls. Because it does contain some gluten, like rye, I use a 50/50 mix of soft wheat to hard wheat in my egg dough recipe for cinnamon rolls, but I don't care for it at that ratio for loaf bread.

Note: If you add vital wheat gluten to your bread, it is technically possible to make a 100% soft wheat bread, however I don't recommend it. It will be crumbly and not hold its rise as well.

**Triticale** (trit-uh-KAY-lee) gets its name from combining parts of the two Latin words for wheat and rye, because that's what it is – a hybrid of those two grains. It seemed like the best of both worlds - a grain with the flavor of rye mixed with the baking quality of wheat, but it flopped in popularity. While it's possible to make a 100% triticale bread, it's a different animal to work with because the dough doesn't behave quite the same. I don't recommend it for beginning bakers, so plan on using it as a blending flour, same as rye. For myself, I can't see the sense of stocking this grain in addition to rye and wheat, although it may be an alterna-tive option for those who are wheat-sensitive.

## Buying and Storing Grains

When I start a new project, sometimes I get so excited that I go a little overboard, which often leads to frustration and confusion. If all of this is brand new to you, take my advice and don't overwhelm yourself by trying to buy several types of grains right away. Start with buying one or two at most, in small quantity, to help you become familiar with how each one acts and tastes in your recipes. As you get a feel for what you like and how much you will use, join-ing a food buying club or co-op will allow you to order grains in bulk for a significantly reduced price.

Be aware that, due to the nature of all agricultural products, grains will vary somewhat in quality from source to source and from year to year. Factors such as weather patterns, the soil in the region where they were grown, and crop conditions all play a part in the overall quality. I've known people who stockpiled grain from a particular year, because it seemed to perform better than that of other years.

## Where to Buy?

Always find out the source of your grains and make sure that they have been double- or triple-cleaned. This helps to ensure that there are no small pebbles or other foreign debris which could ruin your mill and void the warranty. If you get your grain from a local farmer, be sure to pick through it very carefully, as you would when preparing dry beans, removing any foreign matter.

Two popular suppliers for grain are:

- Wheat Montana Farms
  www.wheatmontana.com

- Walton Feed
  www.waltonfeed.com

You, as an individual, can purchase grain directly from these websites (and pay some hefty shipping fees!), or check out their dealer locater to find local dealers, co-ops, or stores to which they supply grain. You can also contact them to find out how to form your own buying group, for lower shipping costs. These are good sites to visit, since they offer quite a bit of additional information, recipes, etc. Click on Walton's site map to see a list of informative articles.

## What Kind to Buy?

For use with the master recipes in this book, I advise starting out with either a hard red or hard white wheat. If you're wheat-sensitive,

then you may prefer to start with Kamut® or spelt. After that, you might try rye and/or soft wheat, but remember that both of these need to be mixed with one of the three base flours (hard wheat, Kamut® or spelt).

Some wheats are known by brand or variety names, which can make matters a little confusing. Wheat Montana's signature hard white spring wheat is called Prairie Gold® and their hard red spring wheat is called Bronze Chief®. Walton Feed sells a variety of hard white wheat called Golden 86.

The next option to consider is how the grain has been treated. Grains may be sold as either:

- Organic

- Certified Chemical-free

- Conventional

Your pocketbook may dictate your decision here, as an organic classification generally means a more expensive product.

According to the USDA's National Organic Program website, "Organic food differs from conventionally produced food in the way it is grown, handled, and processed... produced by farmers who emphasize the use of renewable resources and the conservation of soil and water to enhance environmental quality for future generations...produced without using most conventional pesticides: fertilizers made with synthetic ingredients or sewage sludge; bioengineering, or ionizing radiation. Before a product can be labeled 'organic,' a government-approved certifier inspects the farm where the food is grown to make sure the farmer is following all the rules necessary to meet USDA organic standards."

According to Dutch Valley Foods' website, "Chemical-free is a term used to classify foods that have been produced in a chemical-free environment. Unlike organic farmers, chemical-free farmers are not limited in the types of fertilizers that can be used on their crops. Natural fertilizers can be used such as nitrogen, phosphorous, and potassium, and still result in a chemical-free product if applied at the right time during the growing season. Certified chemical-free products are tested regularly to make sure they are and remain chemical free."

If grain is not labeled as either organic or chemical-free, then it's probably conventional, meaning that it has been treated with industry-standard chemical fertilizers and pesticides.

## How Much to Buy?

This is a little like asking how long a rope is! It depends on how much you need. For bread-making, here are two handy rules of thumb to help you gauge how far your grain will stretch:

- 1 cup grain = 1½ cups flour
- 1 pound grain = 1 loaf bread

Different grains yield a little more or less flour, but this will give you a rough idea.

Next, you'll need to determine how many loaves you plan to eat per week, on average. Be sure to include an extra "loaf" in your calculation if you plan to make any of the delicious variations, such as pizza crust, hamburger buns, or cinnamon rolls. For example, a 50 pound bag of wheat will make about 50 loaves of bread, or 25 loaves of bread and 25 pizza crusts. For a single person eating one of each per week, a bag will last 25 weeks, or about 6 months. For my family of four, I tend to bake the equivalent of six loaves per week, so a bag lasts me about 2 months just for bread. You'll need to add to your order if you want more flour for making pancakes, muffins, and the like.

## What to Expect

Now that you've got your grain, plunge your hands into it and enjoy the feel of it running through your fingers! Look at it closely and get acquainted with it. You may not be sure what your grain is supposed to look like. It should be fairly uniform in color, size, and shape. Some of the kernels may be a little on the greenish side, due to varying stages of ripeness at the time of harvest. Don't worry, this is normal and will not adversely affect your flour. There may be a few kernels here and there with their husks still on them, or small, grain-sized pieces of wheat stalk mixed in. These can be picked out if you wish, along with the occasional black weed seed. If, horror of horrors, you should see a dead bug, pluck him out too. He didn't eat much, and your bread will be sterilized when you bake it.

## How Long to Store?

Most whole grains, when stored correctly, can last indefinitely, since they do not spoil or lose nutritional value until they are broken open by milling. For long-term storage of up to 6-8 years, you'll want to seal your grain in an airtight container with an oxygen absorber (or purchase it already sealed this way) and keep it at a constant temperature of about 70°F. Otherwise, plan to use your open container of grain within a year. If it lasts longer than that, you're probably not eating enough of it!

## Where to Store?

The most important thing is to keep grains cool, dry, and free from pests. They should be stored in a dark location, if possible, and be enclosed in an airtight container. If it's necessary to store bags of grain in a garage or basement with a concrete floor, use a wooden pallet to keep them off the floor and to allow for air circulation. This will prevent moisture from seeping up through the porous concrete. If you store grain in a plastic container, make sure it's food-safe plastic. While there are specialty bags you can purchase to line large containers with, never use a clean garbage bag as a liner, as it's not food-safe.

A few grains which are higher in oil content, such as brown rice, millet, amaranth, and quinoa are more prone to rancidity, and should be used within a few months of purchase. Otherwise, store them in airtight containers (to avoid absorbing moisture) and keep them in the refrigerator or freezer.

All grain, no matter what its type or source, has the potential to contain insects, including their invisible, unhatched eggs. Organically-grown grain is particularly susceptible to this. Depending on the quantity you've purchased, one suggestion to use as a preventative measure is to place your grain in a deep freezer for three days, which should kill any bugs that might be in it. You could use freezer bags and rotate small batches through your freezer until the entire amount has been "treated." This does not kill unhatched eggs, nor guard against future re-infestation, however. The use of several bay leaves inside the grain may help to repel some critters, but it won't kill them. If you have a big problem with pests, and you have the space, you can store grain in freezer bags in the freezer. Take it out a couple of days before you plan to mill it though, because it will have absorbed some moisture in the freezer. Grain must be perfectly dry for milling, or it will cause the mill to clog.

So far, I have had very little trouble with bugs in my grain. One time it was a small container of grain that I used for display purposes at my classes. The grain had been in there for a few years, and I noticed it looked very powdery, like there was flour in it. On closer inspection, I could see tiny Swiss cheese holes in some of the grains. Another time, I noticed some "flour" in the scoop I keep in my grain bucket. I looked a little closer and could see tiny specks crawling around. There are ways to get critters out of your grain and still safely use it, but since this was a fairly small amount of grain, I decided to just pitch it.

Typically, I purchase only enough grain to last for two to three months at a time. Your ordering frequency will depend upon how convenient your grain source is and how much room you have to store it. I purchase 50 pound bags and store them in my kitchen pantry. As soon as I open a new bag, I pour the grain into a 6-gallon food-grade bucket, which holds 45 pounds. The remaining five pounds will go in one of two places. Either I pour it into the hopper of my grain mill, ready for the next time I mill flour, or I store it in canisters or canning jars on a large shelf that my dad custom built for me. I call it my "Wall of Grain." I love the way all the rows of jars look with the contrasting colors and textures of grains and beans, plus it's a visual reminder of the ingredients I should use most often in my cooking.

Most pails come with a standard lid which requires a special lid-removing tool to take them on and a few whacks of a hammer to replace them tightly. I replace that lid with a Gamma Seal Lid. It's a two-piece lid assembly, the bottom ring of which snaps onto the bucket. The ring is threaded, which allows the lid to screw on and off easily and quickly. It has a built-in gasket, creating a watertight, airtight seal, and it fits any 12-inch diameter bucket, from three to seven gallons. No special tools required, and it's open or closed airtight in about 5 seconds!

# Action Steps

1. Which of the base flours have you decided to start with?

   ____ Wheat ____ Kamut ____ Spelt

2. What blending flours would you like to try first (if any)?

   ____Oats/oat flour
   ____Rye
   ____Soft wheat
   Other: _____

3. For flour will you
   ____ mill fresh flour at home
   ____ buy freshly-milled flour
   ____ settle for store-bought flour of unknown age and content

No More Bricks!

Basic Kitchen Tools

Choosing a Grain Mill

Choosing a Mixer

No More Bricks!

## Basic Kitchen Tools

Let me say right away that I am not a fan of cooking gadgets. Every inch of my kitchen is like valuable real estate property, so anything living there had better earn its keep! That means that it has to do a necessary job that nothing else can, or it has to do it so much better or faster that it makes it worth the time to get it out, clean it, and the space to store it. If one tool can do several jobs, I like it even more. It's easier to find things and simpler to clean up when you have less clutter in your way.

I assume that your kitchen is already stocked with the most basic kitchen tools, such as measuring spoons and cups for both dry and liquid measuring, pot holders, spatulas, and the like. However, I have come to rely on a few additional items that bear a little more description.

### Bench Knife

Also known as a bench scraper or dough cutter, it's a 6" x 4" flat blade with a handle across the top edge. Mine has a ruler across the bottom which I use when rolling dough to guage the thickness of it (I'm one of those people who can't guess the measurement of anything without a ruler!), as well as dough proportions. I use it most often for dividing loaves of dough, but

also for cutting, chopping, transferring ingredients, and scraping the counter clean of dried dough. This multi-function tool is so handy that I reach for it often.

### Bowl Scraper

This helps to get all of the dough out of the bowl as well as a number of other household uses. These come in a range of sizes and shapes, but larger ones can be used in place of a bench knife for cutting dough.

### Bread Knife

A good serrated knife is essential for slicing bread into neat, even slices. A plain-edged knife will tear the bread into uneven chunks and make too many crumbs. I like to use an electric knife to make extra thin slices for sandwiches. They're also better for slicing very warm loaves.

### Buckets with Gamma Seal Lids

These are a must for storing grains and other bulk-purchased ingredients. I prefer the 6.5 gallon size bucket because it holds nearly 50 pounds of grain, which is the size bag that I purchase. A standard bucket lid requires a special tool to remove it, but a Gamma Seal lid attaches to any size bucket (with a 12" diameter) from

3.5 to 7 gallons, and eliminates the need for a lid-opening tool. It's a 2-piece system consisting of a snap-on ring and a screw-on lid. The ring attaches firmly to the bucket and includes threads. The lid then easily screws on and off, allowing instant, easy access to its contents.

Condiment Squeeze Bottle

Use this in place of, or in addition to, an oil mister. I fill mine with a mixture of liquid lecithin and vegetable oil for greasing my loaf pans, a mixture that's too thick to spray through the mister without clogging it. I have another squeeze bottle for plain vegetable oil, which I keep close by to squirt on my hands and counter as needed while shaping dough.

## Food Scale

When dealing with multiple loaves' worth of dough, it's a good idea to weigh each one for consistency in appearance as well as in baking times. I weigh not only my loaves, but also my dinner rolls and buns so that some do not dry out while others are underbaked.

## Instant-Read Thermometer

This is absolutely necessary for determining when bread is fully baked, but can also be used for testing the internal temperature of ingredients and bread dough, for troubleshooting purposes. I use a meat thermometer that has a full temperature range from 0° on up. Some of the thermometers I looked at only begin measuring at 120° which isn't low enough.

## Oil Mister

This is a refillable pump to which you can add your favorite oil or custom blend of oils. A few pumps of the handle pressurizes the air inside, making the oil mist like a commercial non-stick spray in an aerosol can.

## Pans

The type of pan you choose will greatly affect not only the appearance and texture of the crust, but also how high it rises and how long it takes to bake. I use several different types, according to the kind of bread I'm making and the crust I want it to have. There are three main points to consider when selecting a pan:

- color or finish

- material and weight

- size

Relatively speaking, the thicker and darker the pan, the more heat it holds, resulting in faster baking with more browning.

### Nonstick or Dark Pans

A nonstick pan, or an older pan that has darkened over time, absorbs heat and will result in a darker crust and take less time to bake. This is my pan of choice for sandwich loaves.

### Shiny Pans

Bright silver metal pans will reflect heat in the oven, causing a lighter crust color and a longer baking time. I prefer these for baking all of my rolls and buns, since I like those items to be softer on the bottom.

## Metal Pans

The choices for metal pans are aluminum, air-insulated aluminum, tinned steel, and stainless steel. Aluminum is a good conductor of heat, but insulated ones are less so, which is why they have the "no-burn" reputation for cookies. Unless aluminum is coated or anodized, it will oxidize to a dull or "spotty" finish.

Steel pans don't conduct heat as well, and will take longer to bake. Stainless steel is usually shiny silver, and it doesn't rust. Tinned steel tends to be darker, and it will rust if not thoroughly dried or if the tin plating is scratched.

Gauge refers to the thickness of metal. The smaller the number, the thicker the pan. Choose heavy-gauge pans to resist warping and promote more even baking.

## Glass Pans

Glass pans heat more slowly than metal, but because they are thick, they hold heat longer. One unique advantage is their transparency, which allows you to monitor browning. I tend to avoid them simply because they're breakable.

## Stoneware Pans

Stoneware pans pull moisture away from food, creating steam for a crispy crust, which makes them ideal for pizza. They can be preheated along with the oven, and because they actually retain heat themselves, they can help to keep the oven temperature more constant and will prevent some heat loss when opening and closing the oven door. Choose a thicker ¾" stone over a ½" one when possible. The use of a pizza peel will allow you to shape free-form breads and pizzas, and then slide them onto the preheated stone inside the oven. Aside from flat baking stones there are stoneware loaf pans and baking pans with lids.

## Pan Size

When baking in loaf pans, it's crucial to match the volume of dough to the size of your pan for tall, rounded loaves that look proportional. For example, if you use 1½ pounds of dough in a standard 9" x 5" pan, your loaf will be short and squat. Put that amount of dough in the next size down, and you have a good-looking sandwich loaf.

- 9" x 5" = 2 pounds
- 8 ½" x 4 ½" = 1½ pounds
- 7 ½" x 3 ½" = 1 pound

To determine what size loaf your recipe makes, a good rule of thumb to follow is that each cup of flour produces ½ pound of bread. So 3 cups of flour = 1½ pounds of dough. Incidentally, that happens to be my preferred size so that's how I've scaled the recipes in this book.

## Parchment Paper

I roll out and shape all kinds of dough on this, especially pizza and stromboli, to help transfer them easily to the oven. I also like to line my baking sheets with it for easy clean-up.

## Pastry Mat/Silicone Mat

Pulling out a pastry mat after my dough has been kneaded provides a clean surface devoid of flour which is desirable for shaping. I have a large plastic one that's imprinted with rolling guides for 8" through 16" circles, and a 2" square grid pattern, making it easy to roll out dough to a specific size and eliminating the guesswork. It stores easily, either rolled up or standing flat in between kitchen cabinet and refrigerator. I also have a smaller silicone mat with similar markings. It has the advantage of not sliding around on the work surface and folding up like a cloth.

## Pizza Peel (paddle)

A long-handled wooden or metal paddle for transferring pizza or free-form loaves onto a preheated baking stone. In a pinch, you could use a rimless cookie sheet instead.

## Rolling Pins

A large barrel heavy duty rolling pin is best for rolling out large pieces of dough for cinnamon rolls and pizza crust. But for smaller jobs, a double-ended pastry roller is convenient, especially when rolling inside a pan. Each end has a roller with a different radius – one rolls the larger middle section, and the other can roll right next to and up the walls of pans.

## Water Spray Bottle

Keep this handy for moistening towels that you use to cover your dough and for spritzing dough while it's in the oven, if you like an extra crisp crust.

## Choosing a Grain Mill

The task of buying a home grain mill can be a daunting one, and no wonder. Many people have never heard of it, and it's not likely to be in any store, not even a fancy kitchen shop.

Because the focus of this book is on speedy breadmaking, I have a strong bias toward mills that are not only speedy, but are convenient to operate and easy to clean too. That means I'm only going to present a very brief outline of the mills available, with an emphasis on the type I prefer. If you would like to study the matter in much more objective detail, I highly recommend the book Flour Power: A Guide to Modern Home Grain Milling by Marleeta F. Basey

(Jermar Press, 2004). It includes an exhaustive checklist you can photocopy for comparing mills of various types and manufacturers.

Before you begin cyber-shopping for a mill, it pays to do your homework and find out exactly what features are the most important to you. In addition to overall size and price, these factors may influence your decision:

- power source
- type of buhr
- texture adjustment
- convenience features

## Power Source

If you have some concern over being able to use your mill during times of power outage, then you'll want to consider whether it uses electrical power or manpower. This will narrow down your field of choices considerably. Mills are typically sold as:

- electric
- manual
- convertible (both manual & electric)

If you opt for a manual or convertible mill, find out how long it will take to mill a cup of flour, and whether it will need to be ground multiple times to produce a texture fine enough for bread flour. Inexpensive manual models are extremely slow and difficult to use, and are not recommended for those with limited physical ability. While there are some very good manual models, they tend to be larger and more expensive.

## Type of Buhr

A buhr (also spelled burr) is the part of the mill that does the actual grinding, so two of them work together in a pair, one spinning against the other. They are discs or plates that can be made of metal, stone (natural or synthetic), or a combination both.

While the words "stone-ground" have a connotation of being natural, and therefore better, 'taint necessarily so. In terms of old, very large millstones which were turned more slowly, the main advantage was that they didn't produce as much heat during milling. For small home mills, most stone buhrs are made of small pieces of synthetic stone and metal and are driven at high speeds, producing as much heat as their all-metal counterparts.

One type of metal buhr contains tiny teeth which rotate very fast and cause grains to "explode" on impact. These are found in electric-only mills called "impact" mills or "micronizing" mills.

## Texture Adjustment

When selecting a mill, it's important to know exactly what you want it to do. Since you're reading a breadmaking book, it may be obvious that you want to make flour, but there is a broad range of flour and grain textures to choose from:

- very fine flour for pastries
- fine to medium flour for bread
- coarse meal for cereal and other baked goods
- coarsely cracked grains
- rolled or flaked grains

While most impact mills can provide a few textures of flour and/or meal, they do not have as wide a range as other types of mills, and they do not crack grains. If your main goal is to make good bread flour and maybe some bean flour and cornmeal, an impact mill will serve you well. If you want very coarse flour or

cracked grain for cereal, you may need either a different type of mill or a special attachment for this purpose.

If you want rolled grain (for cereal or oatmeal bread), then, again, this requires a different type of mill, called a roller or flaker mill. There are a few limited options for small, manual roller/flaker mills which will clamp onto a table-top. These are not as difficult to use as manual models for making flour. Oats are soft and roll easily, but harder grains such as wheat need to be soaked before they can be rolled. There are also two electric mills made by the Family Grain Mill which attach onto either a spiral or stand mixer. One of these will crack, and the other will roll grains.

## Convenience Features

As with any other task, the more convenient and easy it is, the more likely you are to do it. There are a few features that make or break the deal, in my opinion. First, a large grain hopper will let you pour in several pounds of grain without needing to feed it in a little at a time. Next, you need to find out if the mill has to be running before any grain goes into it, because this can cause some mills to clog. If the mill has a pre-cracking chamber, then you can start it whether it has grain in it or not, and that's one less thing to have to think about.

Does the mill have an enclosed container for the freshly-milled flour to go into? If it has only a "spout," and you must supply the bowl, then expect to have flour dust everywhere! The least messy mills will have a bowl fitted with a gasket and at least one type of filter. Without this, you may only want to mill your flour outside, which means you'll be carrying it back and forth, and the weather had better be cooperative. If it does have a flour bowl, check to see what the capacity is. Will you have to empty and refill it to have enough flour for your batch of bread?

For electric mills, try to find someone who owns the mill you're considering, so you can hear firsthand how loud it is. Finally, consider cleaning and storage issues. If possible, read the user's manual in advance of purchase to find out what kind of cleaning and maintenance is required. How long will it take you to set up for milling, and is it easy to get in and out of storage? Some mills clamp onto a table or counter, and some attach to an existing appliance, while others are freestanding. Depending on how often you plan to use it, I highly recommend dedicating some space so you can leave your mill out all the time for easy access.

## What About Blenders?

While there may be blenders on the market that claim they make flour, these do a poor job of grinding flour fine enough for bread. However, if you have a good-quality stand-alone blender, or if your mixer has a blender attachment, it can so some jobs that an average grain mill can't. For example, it can be ideal for grinding nuts and oilseeds into meal or nut butter, and it can make flour from rolled grains. These tasks would clog up a grain mill. Blenders can also do a fair job at coarsely cracking small amounts of grain, though it will not be very uniform in size. See the Tips chapter for more info on how to do this.

The only other way I would recommend using grain in a blender is in conjunction with a lot of liquid, for making a blender batter. Grain can be soaked in liquid, then pureed into pancake or muffin batter, but it requires too much liquid to be suitable for bread.

## Cost Concerns

If the cost of investing in your own mill is prohibitive, try finding a few friends who would be willing to share the cost and rotate the use of a mill with you. You don't need to use it every day. You could mill a month's worth at a time and store it in the freezer. Consider asking your local church or civic groups if they would be willing to purchase and store a mill for communal use.

Don't forget to consider the potential cost to your health from NOT owning a grain mill. When compared to the price of medications, vitamins, fiber supplements, and other synthetic "health foods," a grain mill is a very worthwhile investment.

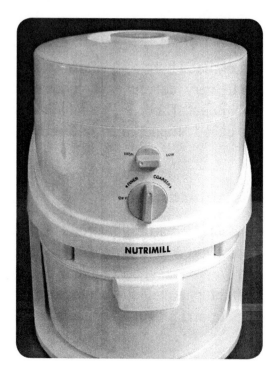

## My Pick

There are a number of pros and cons to each type of mill, which means there's no one perfect solution. Ultimately, you'll have to decide which features are most important to you.

I currently use an impact mill called the Nutrimill, made by Kitchen Resource. After using a few other brands, I chose this one because of its improved design and extra convenience features. It has an air-cooled I like the large grain hopper which holds five pounds of grain, which allows me to walk away while it's running and start prepping my bread ingredients and pans. It takes about 7-10 minutes to fill the bowl with five pounds of flour, which is more than enough for my six-loaf recipe, so I only have to make one batch of flour. I can pull the bowl out and twist open the lid, while the motor is supported by the machine base. This is much easier than some models, whose motors are encased in the "lid," making it more difficult to remove. The sealed bowl has a filter and separator cup which capture the flour dust, and its quiet operation is no louder than a typical vacuum cleaner – a real improvement over some others I've had that required earplugs. Once my dough is kneading, I'll place the leftover flour into the freezer for pancakes or muffins. Cleanup is a breeze. I bought a paintbrush which I keep exclusively to whisk out the inside of the bowl and filter cup – no washing required. That's all there is to it; it's ready for use the next time.

I would no more be without my grain mill than I would my stove or refrigerator. It's become an integral part of my kitchen, and has transformed the way we eat, adding a new level of taste, nutrition, and just plain fun to my baking.

## Choosing a Mixer

Are you on the fence about what to use to mix your bread? I think I can help you narrow down your choices pretty quickly. It's really just a matter of deciding how much and how often you plan to bake. The first thing you should do is think about how many loaves of bread you need to last your family for an average week. Remember, you'll need more than your current usage of store-bought bread, because homemade tastes so much better that you'll eat more of it. To help you figure out your "magic number," turn right now to the Action Steps at the end of this chapter, and look over Steps 3, 4, 5, & 6. Think about those answers for a few minutes,

and then come back here. Go ahead. Go right now. I promise, I'll wait...

Got those answers firmly in mind? If so, you might be ready to skip right to the machine you've already chosen – the one that meets your quantity and frequency requirements. Maybe you already own one or more machines, and your budget demands that it be put to use, whether it fits your lifestyle or not. Or maybe you're hung up on the idea that you "ought" to make bread by hand instead of machine. Let's address that first, before launching into more specifics about the different types of mixers.

## Man vs. Machine

Using a mixer to make bread is a great luxury, one that I am so glad I finally allowed myself to have. Since my breadmaking experiences as a child were done by hand kneading, I used to think that was the only way to do it. Even as an adult, it seemed more "authentic" to make bread by hand. I've come a long way, baby!

It's been said that a new baker should make her first loaf of bread by hand, in order to learn to make bread by "feel" so she can understand and appreciate the transformation of sticky goo into a smooth, elastic dough. Once she has mastered this, then she has supposedly earned the right to switch to a faster machine method. Hmm. Why don't we extend that line of logic to other basic household chores? Maybe when you do your next load of laundry, you should have the experience of hiking to the nearest creek and beating shirts and socks with a rock to get them clean. This will teach you to understand and appreciate your washing machine, right? Don't get me wrong; I have nothing against those who choose to make bread by hand, as long as they have the time and find it to be an enjoyable experience. I just think it's much easier to learn and more efficient to make bread by machine. I also don't think that a hand kneader who's trying to feed a family will consistently take the time and effort required to make enough bread this way.

Making bread by machine isn't a completely automatic process anyway; there's plenty of opportunity to get your hands in the dough, minus the sticky mess, thank you. Believe me, even after years of making bread in my mixer, I still get a thrill each time I take a silky-soft, perfect ball of dough from it. I can even get a little stress relief by giving the dough a few good whacks on the counter to deflate it before I lovingly shape it and nestle it into its pan. That's enough personal contact for me.

## Mixer Myths

Even though there are several types of appliances you can use to make bread, I'm going to refer to them all as "mixers" from here on out, to keep things simple (for me, at least). When deciding which one to purchase (or which deserves to continue living in your kitchen!) It helps to break them down by type, taking into account other possible functions of the machine for maximum value and efficient use of space. There are five basic types of mixers, and since I'm in charge of this book, I've listed them in order of my own personal preference:

- Spiral Mixer

- Stand (Planetary) Mixer

- Food Processor

- Bread Machine

- Hand Mixer

I'll be giving a brief description of each a little later, along with the pros and cons, as I see them. But first, there are some basic "rules" you need to know before you go out and buy one. Even if you already own the mixer you'll be using for bread, please don't skip this next part,

because it could drastically impact the lifespan of your machine.

Here's a newsflash. There's a lot of misinformation and hype involved in advertising. If you want to save yourself a lot of time, trouble, and money, you have to know what function you're trying to accomplish and what features to look for before you ever go shopping. Aside from knowing your baking frequency and quantity numbers, these are the specs you need to look at to be able to accurately comparison shop for a mixer:

- horsepower

- torque (transmission)

- capacity

But unfortunately, all you will actually find is:

- wattage

- capacity

Notice that wattage is not the same thing as horsepower. And torque, who talks about that? What does that even mean? Don't worry, we'll get to that.

## What's Up With Watts?

Manufacturers love to brag about machine wattage, claiming it's more powerful than others with lower wattage. While there is something to be said for the amount of wattage, it's really not enough information to base a decision on alone. The fact is, it doesn't tell you much about how the machine will perform.

I hope I don't insult your intelligence, but, if you're like me, you don't know much 'bout watts, torque, transmissions, or any of that mechanical stuff. Much to my husband's dismay, I don't really understand how my car works either, just that when I start it, it goes. So I had to do some real investigative digging in this area, scouring manufacturer's websites, reading reviews by consumer advocate groups and test kitchens, and wading through endless rants and raves from mixer owners of all types and brands in bakers' forums. Armed with all these facts and comparison charts, I did the only thing I knew to do next and, uh, asked my husband to explain it all to me in plain English. I should really have him write this part of the book, but since he can't type, I'll do my best.

Being a car guy, whenever David wants to teach me something, more often than not he will use some kind of car analogy. So to help my feeble brain understand all this technical mumbo jumbo, he relates it to something a little more familiar to me, like shopping for a car. Of course, I'm not "into" cars much either, but I've heard a lot about something called a Corvette; it's supposed to be really fast. Following his advice, I look at the manufacturer's website to see what the specs are. Since I live way out in the boonies, one of the first things I look for is how good the gas mileage is. Gas mileage.... hey, wait a minute, that's kind of like wattage. Simply put, a watt is a unit of measurement for how much electricity something uses. It's like the gasoline a car uses, expressed in miles per gallon (mpg). I think we're on to something here. The Corvette claims a highway mileage rating of 26 mpg. Next, we need to compare that to another vehicle. So I look up an SUV, a Chevy Suburban, and it gets 21 mpg. At first glance, the mileage ratings, or wattages, if you will, are similar. Or are they? Pretend I've never seen or driven either one of these before. Does the gas mileage number alone describe how fast the vehicle can go, how it maneuvers sharp turns, how much of a load it can haul, or how it handles in the snow? Nope. Let's look a little closer. A Corvette seats two people only. It's small and light, and goes fast. Man, I'll look good in that - I can already feel the wind blowing in my hair! But wait a second. I've got a family of four, a big dog, and we need to pull a cargo trailer to the different locations where I attend conventions and teach classes. That's not a job for a Corvette. On the other hand, the Suburban is roomy enough for up to 6 people or more, has lots of cargo space, and a big trailer hitch for hauling. Even though both vehicles get similar gas mileage (wattage), they're built for different purposes.

The only time wattage is really useful is in comparing mixers of the same brand and design. But if you're looking at mixers from different manufacturers, you're comparing apples to oranges. The bottom line is, no manufacturer tells you the measure of output (horsepower); they only tell you the input (wattage).

## Got Torque?

Like a lever can lift heavy objects with less effort, a transmission can multiply torque, or strength. If you had a mixer with a 4000 watt motor, but it didn't have the right transmission, you couldn't beat an egg in the thing, let alone bread dough. The mixer's transmission is a series of gears that transforms the high speed power from the motor into high-torque power to turn the dough hook. Horsepower makes things go fast, but torque is strength; it's what pushes heavy things. In our car example, the Corvette had horsepower. But hook a heavy trailer onto the back, and it can't budge. That's because it doesn't have the transmission (torque) to pull a heavy load.

Once again, the problem with rating mixers by wattage is that the amount of power the motor uses has little to do with the ability of the dough hook to push through heavy, whole grain dough.

## Capacity Matters

Most mixers will advertise their breadmaking capacity in terms of the number of cups of flour or the number of loaves of bread. This can be very misleading, because those measurements are almost always referring to all-purpose white flour or white bread only! You must read the fine print to determine how many cups of whole grain flour (sometimes called "specialty flour") or how many whole grain loaves are recommended. In the case of loaves, try to find out how much those loaves weigh. One popular "professional" model with a hefty price tag boasts that it makes eight loaves of bread, but closer inspection reveals that those are only one-pound loaves of white bread! I recommend going to the manufacturer's website, where you should be able to download the user's manual, complete with recipes. Look specifically at the whole wheat recipes and their yields. Often these will be different from what's claimed on the box. Bingo!

The second part of the capacity challenge is to realize that, if you regularly operate it at its maximum ability, it will likely have a shorter lifespan than a mixer used at less intensity. So, if you plan to make bread regularly, you should buy a mixer with more capacity and strength than you need, as it will greatly increase its longevity by not overtaxing it.

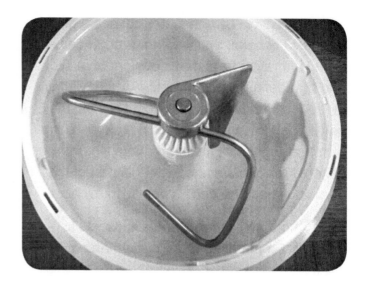

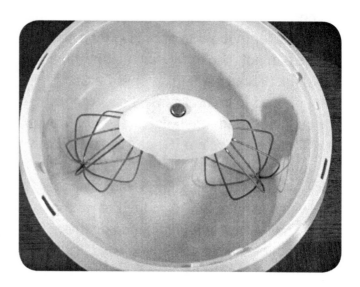

## Spiral Mixer (e.g. Bosch or Electrolux)

A spiral mixer is probably the one of the bunch that you are least familiar with. Spiral mixers get their name from either their spiral shaped dough hooks or the fact that they have bowls that spin instead of the beaters, like stand mixers do. They are engineered to handle a much larger amount of heavy dough, up to hundreds of pounds, making them ideal for bakeries and other large scale kitchens. Of course, we're only going to consider models that are suitable (not to mention affordable) for home use.

No More Bricks!

The two most popular brands are made by Bosch and Electrolux (formerly marketed under the name Magic Mill). In most parts of the country, these are only available for purchase from authorized online dealers, so you won't find them in retail stores. One very nice feature of these mixers is that the view down into the mixing bowl is unobstructed by an overhanging motor "head," since its motor is found in the base of the unit. This also helps to makes it lightweight and more compact.

The model I personally use is the Bosch Universal Plus. This is the machine that I saw for the first time at my friend Kathy's house. At the time, she had owned hers for over 15 years, and had used it regularly for bread and other mixing functions, as well as various optional attachments which it powers. Since then, I've met many people who have Bosches that are going on 20 years old, and, like the Energizer Bunny, still going. Bosch claims the average lifespan is 17 years, and I believe it, based on what I've seen so far.

The Bosch model is a little different from the other spirals in that the bowl does not spin. Rather, it has a large, three-armed dough hook that extends upward from the base through the center of the bowl. It has a belt-driven transmission and is a proven performer with whole grain bread dough. Despite this, the entire machine is very compact and weighs only 13 pounds, about half that of a typical stand mixer! Its twin beaters and paddles work in the traditional "planetary" motion, by way of snapping into a coupler which rotates on the the center column. The beaters work so efficiently that they can whip a single egg white into 1½ cups of meringue.

The Electrolux has an 8-quart bowl that spins, making use of a stationary bowl scraper and an agitator. It will also make six loaves, possibly more, as it's rated for up to 15 pounds of dough.

Since most ovens will not accommodate more than six loaf pans, it wouldn't be useful to make more than that unless you have the luxury of a double oven. It also has a separate mixing bowl with beaters that work in the traditional planetary motion.

In comparing the two brands, I chose the Bosch because it's easier to use, while the Electrolux has a bit of a learning curve, due to its adjustable tension arm. The Bosch was also the least expensive, not only of those in its own class, but even of those which had a lower capacity and strength. The 6.5 quart bowl easily handles my largest recipe for nine pounds of dough (six 1½ pound loaves), although it's rated for up to 12 pounds of dough.

Aside from that, I mainly chose the Bosch based on enthusiastic testimonials of friends in our homeschooling network who have relied on them for many years. Since I purchased my Bosch, I've been thrilled with it, and don't know how I ever got along without it before. In addition to making bread, I also use it for mixing tortilla dough, cookies, cakes, meringue, or anything else that a traditional stand mixer does.

With my busy schedule, I don't have time to make bread three to four times a week to keep up with the needs of my family, so I've chosen the most efficient machine I can find to help me out. It enables me to make all of the different types of bread we eat during a week's time, including sandwiches, pizza, sweet rolls, etc. In combination with a grain mill, it's like having a mini bakery in your own home. Everyone I know who is really serious about preparing whole grain breads for a family has a spiral mixer. It just is THE machine for the job.

**Maximum Loaves per Batch:**

Up to six, or more

## What I like:

Built for bulk and speed; dependable for prolonged and heavy use.

## What I don't like:

While the beaters handle the tiniest jobs with ease, when using the dough hook it's not really suitable for making a single loaf of bread only. You need to make at least two loaves, and preferably three for best kneading results. This is only a factor for me when I want to test out a new recipe, since I usually prefer to make three to six loaves at a time anyway.

## Bottom Line:

The spiral mixer opens up a whole new world of breadmaking by enabling you to make dough in bulk. It should last for many years of continued, heavy use, making it a very worthwhile investment for the frequent bread baker.

## Planetary Stand Mixer

The familiar stand mixer's motor is located above the mixing bowl and is the place from which its single beater, paddle, or dough hook suspends down into the bowl. The planetary motion means that the mixing implement spins as it rotates, the same way planets orbit the sun. Available in a number of sizes and styles, it's engineered more for light mixing jobs and kneading white flour dough. It's very important to read the instructions for your specific model, because trying to mix more whole grain dough than the mixer is rated for can lead to stripping the gears and burning out the motor prematurely.

Probably the most recognizable brand name of stand mixers is Kitchen Aid, but there are many others. Bosch also makes a very affordable mixer of this type, called the Compact, that will mix up to three loaves.

## Maximum Loaves per Batch:

One to three, depending on model and age of machine

## What I Like:

It's easy to use, and is familiar to most cooks

## What I Don't Like:

It's not suitable for larger jobs or frequent, heavy kneading, plus it takes longer to mix and knead.

## Bottom Line:

Stand mixers can be an option for those who have time to bake more often or who don't need as much quantity. If you do use it regularly for whole grain bread, don't expect it to last more than a year or two before it needs replacement. One probable exception to this is the Bosch

Compact, which is designed for whole grain bread dough.

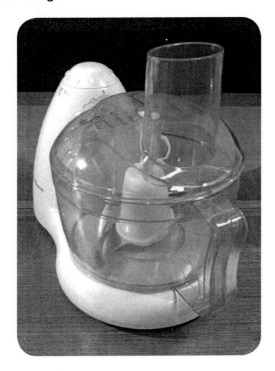

## Food Processor

The food processor is a whiz at making bread very quickly, as little as 45-60 seconds for kneading! Even if you mess up the dough, (and it's far from foolproof) you have very little time and cost of ingredients invested. You can also make successive batches in roughly the same amount of time as it would take to knead one batch in a stand mixer, if you have all your ingredients premeasured and ready to go. However, the caveat to all this speed is that the machine creates a lot more heat, and it's also very easy to overknead the dough. You should expect to have to throw out a few batches of dough while you are learning with this machine.

Again, be sure to check your specific model's instructions for the maximum amount of whole grain flour or dough that is recommended. As with stand mixers, even if the volume capacity of the bowl is large enough for multiple loaves,

that does not mean that the motor is strong enough to turn through stiff whole grain dough.

### Maximum Loaves per Batch:

One

### What I Like:

The food processor is a very versatile kitchen appliance. Provided it has enough power, mixing and kneading is super speedy; overall size makes it easy to use and store.

### What I Don't Like:

It takes a lot more practice to get the dough just right, without overworking or overheating the dough. Making successive batches of bread requires measuring ingredients multiple times, and could cause strain or overheating of the motor. You need a higher-end model (that means more $$) to get good performance with heavy bread dough.

### Bottom Line:

If you have a beefy enough model, this is by far the fastest way to mix and knead a single loaf of bread, but it can be a little tricky to get the hang of. If your model is more on the wimpy side, save it for chopping and puréeing, and invest in a mixer instead.

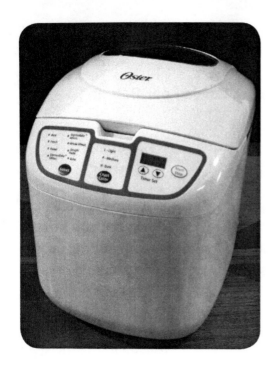

## Bread Machine

The bread machine, also called an auto bakery, is just that. An all-in-one-mixing-kneading-rising-baking machine. Most models include a delay timer so you can set it to finish baking fresh bread just before you wake up or when you get home from work. It would seem to be the ideal choice for busy bakers, and no doubt, for some it is. You may be surprised that it's low on my list, but the fact is that I just don't like 'em! I had one in my kitchen for years, but after the initial novelty wore off, I used it seldom.

While bread machines do a passable job for white bread, they really aren't equipped to handle heavy whole grain dough. The initial mixing is very slow, if you're waiting to add flour to achieve the proper liquid-to-flour ratio, as I recommend. Nevertheless, it can be done. Using a flexible spatula to help move the flour toward the paddle may help to speed up the mixing process. Once the dough is properly mixed, you can allow it to finish the rest automatically, or you may opt to make use of just the dough cycle. I think baking the loaf in a conventional oven produces a better end product than bak-

ing it inside the machine, where I never found the crust to be to my liking, no matter what setting was chosen. Otherwise, try to be present to take the loaf out as soon as it completes the baking cycle, or it will get soggy in the pan.

Note: One of these machines seems to out-perform all the others: the Japanese-made Zojirushi bread machine has two mixing paddles, makes a traditionally-shaped loaf, and works well for whole grain bread. However, the cost is at least twice that of other brands.

### What I Like:

I'll admit it's convenient to pour everything in and walk away while the machine does it all, provided that you're pleased with the results. Cleanup is minimal.

### What I Don't Like:

The tiny mixing blade is slow and inefficient. The machine is large, making storage an issue, but the yield is only one awkwardly-shaped loaf at a time.

### Bottom Line:

There are other appliances which are more versatile and do a more efficient job of mixing & kneading, while taking up much less kitchen space.

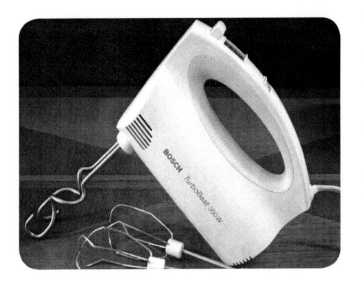

**What I Don't Like:**

Can't finish the job; not useful for more than initial mixing of one or two loaves

**Bottom Line:**

If no other mixer is available, using a hand mixer can reduce the amount of kneading and rising time when making bread by hand.

## Hand Mixer

This was the only mixer I owned for many years, but I never realized that it could be useful in starting bread dough. It works well in the initial stage of mixing, since it helps to distribute the yeast throughout the mixture and begins to activate the gluten. But as you begin to add flour, discontinue use of the mixer as soon as it begins to have difficulty turning through the dough. At that point, you'll have to finish mixing and kneading by hand.

Note: Bosch makes a good-quality hand mixer that includes regular beaters, plus dough hooks. You still need to do some hand kneading, but it works harder than any other hand mixer I've seen.

**Maximum Loaves per Batch:**

Zero - it can't finish kneading a loaf unaided

**What I Like:**

The compact size makes it handy to use and store, and cleanup is a breeze – pop the beaters in the dishwasher. Very inexpensive and versatile for small jobs.

# Action Steps

1. Do you have all the tools you need or want to bake bread?

____Bench Knife

____Bowl Scraper

____Bread Knife

____Buckets w/ G.S. Lids

____Condiment Bottle

____Cooling Racks

____Food Scale

____Instant Thermometer

____Oil Mister

____Pans: Baking Stone

____Pans: Sheet/Jellyroll

____Pans: Loaf

____Pans: Pizza

____Parchment Paper

____Pastry Mat

____Pizza Peel

____Rolling Pins

____Water Spray Bottle

2. Which features of a grain mill are most important to you?

____Speed of operation

____Grain Hopper

____Flour Bowl & Dust Filters

____Electric power

____Manual/Convertible power

____Low price

____Appearance

____Easy to Clean & Maintain

____Convenience of Operation

____Heat Control

____Texture Options – Fine to Coarse

____Cracking Grains

____Rolling/Flaking Grains

____Other: _____

3. Decide, on average, how many loaves of bread you need to make per week, and put the number in the blank. If you're not sure, scan the recipe section for variation ideas. Be sure to count a "loaf" for each of the following:

____Sandwiches & Toast

____Hamburger Buns

____Pizza Crusts

____Dinner Rolls

____Sweet Rolls

____Bread Bowls

____Meals in a Loaf

____Giving Away

____Other: _____

4. Total number of loaves from above _____

5. How often per week do you have time to bake?

_____

6. Which machine will help you keep up with this realistically?

____Spiral Mixer (up to 6 or more loaves per batch)

____Stand Mixer (1-2 loaves per batch)

____Food Processor (1 loaf per batch)

____Bread Machine (1 loaf per batch)

____Hand Method (1-2 loaves per batch)

Six Basic Ingredients

Two Special Ingredients

Mysterious Gluten

No More Bricks!

## Six Basic Ingredients

Yeast bread really only requires four ingredients: flour, water, yeast, and salt. But for most American bread recipes, you will find these six basic ingredients in one related form or another:

- water
- flour
- salt
- yeast
- oil
- sugar

## Water or Liquid

All breads must have some liquid to moisten the flour. This is usually water, but could also include milk, juice, broth, etc. for additional flavoring. Water contributes to a crisper crust, while milk tenderizes bread and helps it to keep a little longer. Milk also promotes deeper browning of the crust, due to its fat and sugar content (lactose).

## Flour

This can be any combination of grains, but for soft, light bread that's not too dense, you need to use a wheat-family flour. These are discussed at length in the Grains & Flours chapter.

## Salt

Not only does it add flavor to the bread, but salt's vital role is to control the growth of the yeast. If you forget the salt, or do not have enough, the yeast will grow too much and rise higher than it can be supported. Some recipes call for adding the salt last, after allowing the yeast a bit of a head start in fermenting before the salt can retard it. I did this for a while, but so often ended up forgetting to put the salt in at all, that I gave up and began adding it along with the other dry ingredients. I noticed no major difference.

You can use any kind of salt you like, as long as it's not too coarse, so that it doesn't damage the gluten. I use sea salt, but I especially like to use RealSalt®, which contains no chemical additives or anti-caking agents. Table salt and some sea salts are, like white sugar, highly refined and bleached until they're pure white. Bet you never thought of that before, eh? I hadn't either! Salts can also contain many additives, including dextrose (sugar)! I don't use Realsalt® all the time, because it's quite a bit more expensive. You can probably find it easily, as it's becoming more widely available in grocery stores and health food stores. For more information, check out their website at www.realsalt.com.

## Yeast

Yeast is a living organism that is present in the air. You can capture your own yeast as is the process with sourdough breads, or you can purchase it packaged commercially. Yeast requires warm liquid and food (flour or sugar) to make it "bloom" or activate, much as a seed needs water and soil to sprout. The yeast uses the sugar for energy and begins to reproduce rapidly, giving off alcohol waste and little carbon dioxide "burps," which produce the familiar bubbles and foam. This reproduction process is called fermentation. The longer the yeast ferments in your dough, the more flavor it will impart to the bread. It needs to be evenly distributed in the dough during mixing to work properly.

There are three types of baker's yeast: compressed yeast cakes, active dry yeast, and instant yeast (often the words fast, rapid, or quick are a part of the trademark name). Don't confuse any of these with brewer's yeast or nutritional yeast.

Compressed cake yeast is also called "wet yeast" or "fresh yeast." It's not used much by home bakers anymore, as it's highly perishable and has to be stored in the refrigerator, with a shelf life of only about 8 weeks.

Active dry yeast is the product that most of us are familiar with. It has been dehydrated with high heat and coaxed into a semi-dormant state. The high heat causes many of the yeast cells to die, which surround the remaining live cells, protecting them. This is why you must "proof" the yeast first, to dissolve the outer dead cells and activate the live cells underneath. Because of the number of dead cells, you need to use more active dry yeast. The water temperature must be carefully measured, from 105 to 115 degrees, warm enough to encourage yeast growth, but cool enough that it won't be killed. After a few minutes there should be a noticeable amount of bubbles and foam, at which point it is ready to use.

Instant yeast (also called bread machine yeast) is the yeast of choice for most bakers because it does not require proofing. Instant yeast is dried at lower temperatures, so the proportion of live cells is much greater, allowing you to use up to 25% less instant yeast than active dry yeast. This contributes to smaller individual granules which absorb liquid more quickly and can be added directly to the dry ingredients and mixed immediately. Because it's not being added directly to the liquid first, but is surrounded by flour, the liquid temperature can be higher (120° – 130°) which contributes additional warmth to the dough, helping it to rise faster. A small amount of ascorbic acid (vitamin C) has also been added to aid in rising.

More yeast is required in whole grain breads than for white breads, because the flour is heavier, requiring more strength to raise the dough.

Increasing the amount of yeast in a recipe will make it rise faster and higher, but too much can contribute to an overly yeasty taste and over-proofing – dough that rises too high to support itself.

It is significantly cheaper to buy yeast in bulk, in a one pound package, as opposed to the individual strip packets or the 4 ounce jars. I use SAF (SAF is short for LeSaffre Corporation) instant yeast, made by Red Star, which is highly favored by professional bakers. One ¼ ounce package of yeast is equivalent to about 2 ¼ to 2 ½ teaspoons, or a scant tablespoon.

## Fats

Fat adds flavor and makes bread that is moist, tender, and with better keeping quality. It helps to lubricate the gluten strands, making them easier to expand.

I use canola oil in my recipes, but any oil will work. I think olive oil has too strong of a flavor for everyday sandwich bread, but I know of many who prefer to use it.

A recipe calling for shortening or butter provides the same function as oil. I prefer unsalted

No More Bricks!

butter for baking as opposed to salted butter. Because it's prone to rancidity, I keep it in the freezer until I'm ready to use it. Many times salted butter has already turned rancid, and the salt just covers up the taste.

I don't feel margarine is suitable for any kind of baking, but if you do use it, make sure it is not "diet" margarine, where the first ingredient is water. Whenever possible, I try to avoid using shortening.

People often ask if they can omit the oil entirely to reduce or eliminate the fat content. The answer is yes, since it's not required. Personally, I feel that I use such a small amount (equivalent to about 2 tablespoons per loaf) that there is not a significant amount per slice to worry about, calorie-wise. You should experiment to find a level that is satisfactory to you.

According to the Kansas Wheat Commission, 80% of the population mistakenly believes that bread is fattening. While some breads, such as croissants, certainly do have a higher fat content, typical sandwich bread does not. Whole grain breads, with their high fiber content, are known to aid in weight control by making you feel full, so you will naturally consume fewer calories.

## Sugar (or other sweetener)

This is another area where you can really personalize your bread, not only in the type of sweetener used, but in the amount. The purpose of sugar or sweetener is to act as food for the yeast, add flavor, and aid in browning of the crust.

The choices in this category include: white sugar, brown sugar, molasses, honey, or any of the less-refined sugars, such as sucanat or evaporated cane juice crystals.

Many people ask why I do not always use honey in my bread recipes. The reason is partly due to cost, and partly for nutritional purposes. First, honey is much more expensive than sugar. Second, I would rather spread a little honey on my baked bread than to bake it inside the loaf. This is because there are at least 165 known nutrients in honey, including amino acids, enzymes, vitamins, minerals, and phytochemicals (trace nutrients found in plants), many of which are destroyed by heat. This is why I only use local, raw honey, unpasteurized and unfiltered, which has not been heated to levels that destroy these nutrients.

There are some benefits to using honey in your bread. Honey is hygroscopic (hygro, not hydro), which means it draws moisture to itself. This causes the bread to stay moist longer. Because it is itself a liquid, it will slightly affect the amount of flour used in the recipe. This is not a problem, as you will be learning how much flour to add by feel instead of by measurement anyway. You will just add a little more flour to compensate. Honey is more concentrated than sugar, so it takes less honey to equal the same amount of sugar in terms of sweetness. You can guesstimate about 25% less honey than sugar, but here is the official conversion:

- 1 cup sugar = ¾ cup honey and Reduce 2 tablespoon liquid in recipe

_____

- 1 cup honey = 1¼ cup sugar and Add 2 tablespoon liquid to recipe

When I don't use honey, I prefer to use evaporated cane juice crystals (ECJ) or sucanat. Sucanat stands for SUgar CAne NATural. These are types of sugar that are less refined than table sugar, and are not chemically bleached. Florida Crystals is one popular brand and is now commonly available in most grocery stores. To get the best possible price, buy these sugars in bulk from a food buying club or co-operative.

## Two Special Ingredients

There are two additional ingredients I use in my bread that are not called for in most recipes: Vital Wheat Gluten and Dough Enhancer®. They are both optional and can easily be omitted from any of my recipes, but I recommend them highly. The best way to determine whether or not they make a difference in your bread is to make one batch with these ingredients and one batch without. They can also be used independently of each other.

### Vital Wheat Gluten

Many years ago, I purchased a bag of gluten from an Amish bulk foods store. I didn't know exactly what it was, but I had heard it had something to do with making bread better. I put it in my fridge and left it for a long time, since I didn't know what to do with it and wasn't making much bread at the time. Now I know that it's a bread baker's best friend!

You're probably familiar with commercially available bread flour, which is a high-gluten flour. Having a can of vital wheat gluten on hand can transform any flour into bread flour. Just make

sure it says "vital" on the label; plain old "gluten flour" is not the same thing.

The next section explains what exactly gluten is, and its role in making a perfect loaf of bread.

It is possible to make your own gluten. My kids and I actually made it one day as an experiment, by stirring flour and water together vigorously for several minutes, then rinsing off the starch. What was left looked and felt like a mass of very thin, clear threads, similar to corn silk. However, to make it into a usable product for bread, we would have then had to bake the rinsed strands, grind them into a course powder, dry that, and then regrind it into a fine powder. Too much work! But it did help to make sense of all that I had read about it. Instead of just believing it was there, I could actually see it.

Commercially prepared gluten is available, and is a real convenience. I buy mine in a 27 ounce can and add one tablespoon for each loaf of bread the recipe yields, so the can will make about 76 loaves of bread, at a cost of just a few cents per loaf.

Again, this is an optional ingredient, and if you're using a high-protein wheat, is not absolutely required. However, I've tried making bread without it a few times, and my family can always tell the difference. My husband especially complains that the bread is not as pliable and soft for making sandwiches. I notice that it takes longer for the bread to rise, and it doesn't rise as high, so it's denser. Not quite a brick, but too close for comfort.

Because vital wheat gluten is a product made from refined white flour, it might be considered by some as a compromise to add it to 100% whole grain bread, but for just a tablespoon per loaf, I see it as an insignificant amount to worry about. It does dramatically improve the bread to the point that we eat a lot more of it on a regular basis, which is healthier in the long run. If you choose to use only one "special ingredient" in your bread, then I highly recommend that it be vital wheat gluten.

## Dough Enhancer®

Sometimes called a dough conditioner, improver, or stabilizer, this is the other special ingredient that I add to my bread. As I said before, it is technically optional. However, it contributes softness and lightness to breads. It strengthens the cell walls of the dough, and also helps in the rising process, with a small boost of yeast and ascorbic acid (vitamin C).

Not all dough conditioners are created equally. Be sure to check the ingredients listed. I have seen some listing the first ingredients (meaning the highest relative quantity) as white flour and sugar!

The one I use comes in a 21 ounce can. Used at a rate of one teaspoon per loaf, it will yield 200 loaves. It is a shelf-stable dry powder, and will keep for up to 18 months, according to the manufacturer. It contains: whey, soy lecithin, tofu powder, citric acid, sea salt, corn starch, ascorbic acid (Vitamin C), enriched flour, and dry yeast. Don't worry about the minute amount of "enriched" flour near the end of the list. Remember that you will be adding only one teaspoon to an entire loaf of bread! There could only be a few granules of white flour in that teaspoon, since there is a larger concentration of all the other ingredients that come before it in the list. However, if it bothers you, feel free to leave it out.

There are other ways to improve bread dough, including recipes for homemade dough enhancers. You may have seen some ingredients, especially in older cookbooks or recipes, which seemed to be an odd "flavoring" for bread. Using the water from boiled potatoes and/or mashed potatoes, lemon juice, ginger, buttermilk or other milk products, and soy or garbanzo bean flour are examples of these. Crushed vitamin C tablets or granules, liquid or powdered lecithin, and malt powder are also examples of ways to condition bread dough. These are all worth considering, if you have the time and desire to experiment.

## Mysterious Gluten

Gluten is the protein that is unique to wheat and its relatives, spelt and Kamut®, and to a lesser degree, rye and barley. It's not exactly an ingredient in these grains per se, but the protein compounds which produce gluten are. They're called gliadin and glutenin, and under the right conditions, they bind together to form gluten. It's up to you to produce those "right conditions," and I'll explain how in a moment.

When we talk about protein content in grains, it can be confusing, because there are many different kinds of protein. Oats and quinoa are high in protein, but so are milk and meat. None of those kinds of protein will aid in breadmaking, however.

Even though the gluten-forming compounds are naturally present in wheat, the level fluctuates because of differences in wheat varieties, growing seasons, and weather conditions. Commercial mills have laboratories that run tests on each lot of grain they receive to identify the protein and moisture content. They can then blend different varieties and sources of wheat to produce many types of flours with consistent levels of gluten for assorted baking purposes. Since I don't have a test tube lab in my kitchen to rate the quality of my wheat, I add a little concentrated gluten as an insurance policy.

Having enough gluten present in your bread is only half the battle though. Before we move on to the second half of the gluten double-feature, let's get up close and personal with gluten and see it in action. I promise you, it's worth the extra time to get your head wrapped around this concept.

The word "gluten" itself comes from the Latin word for "glue." Back in kindergarten, you probably mixed white flour and water together to make a kind of glue for papier-mâché creations. However, in terms of breadmaking, gluten is not exactly a binding agent. When properly developed, it provides the structure or "skeleton" of the bread. If you've ever made a bread brick, chances are it was because of a lack of gluten.

I'm a visual person. I have to see things in order to understand them fully, and as a teacher, I'm a firm believer in visual aids, 3-D models, and hands-on experiments. I just love to take an abstract concept and relate it to something more familiar, so that's what I'm going to do now. First, I assign you to do this little experiment on your own. Take a teaspoon or so of vital wheat gluten and add a tiny bit of water to it. Stir it briefly and watch as it transforms into a rubbery ball. (Incidentally, if you're not sure whether you have vital wheat gluten as opposed to high-gluten flour, since they look similar, you can do this same test to see if you get rubber.)

Don't throw away your gluten ball just yet, because we'll refer back to it in the next chapter. For now, we can compare that rubbery stuff to the latex used to make balloons. In my bread classes, I use a balloon as a model to illustrate how gluten works. You know how sometimes it's hard to blow up a balloon? So what do you do? You stretch it back and forth several times, kinda like kneading. Well, not exactly, but work with me here. Next, when you blow into the balloon, it expands, trapping the air inside and giving shape to it. This is how gluten performs in your bread – it gives shape and form. The action of the yeast is like blowing air; it creates a force that expands the dough. The gluten stretches with the air bubbles that the yeast gives off (carbon dioxide), trapping them so that they don't escape into the air, and forming the familiar loaf shape. During baking, as soon as the internal temperature of the dough reaches 140°, the yeast dies. That means there's no longer any pressure being exerted on the walls of the bread, nothing to keep pushing it up and outward. At this point, the bread will begin to fall, unless (TA-DA!) the gluten framework is present. As the yeast has given up the ghost, the gluten has been solidifying during baking. The stretchy strands that you noticed during kneading have done their magic work, and are now firmly supporting the risen loaf of bread!

Okay, here's the part I told you was coming, the second half of the gluten mystery: developing the right conditions for gluten to form. (But wait, in case you got lost in my long-winded explanation of what the first half was, it's just making sure you have enough gluten present to work with - that's why we add a little extra.) Now, back to the second half. Gluten is a little like yeast, in that it needs two things to activate it. Yeast needs warm liquid and food. Gluten needs liquid too, and you saw what happened when we did that, it made rubber. Actually, that could be a little misleading, because, if you remember, we were using concentrated, pre-made gluten. It doesn't happen so instantly while in its natural state in the flour. Which brings us to the second part of gluten activation. It's not food, like yeast needs, it's agitation. In other words, it needs to be needed, I mean kneaded. Kneading helps to "untangle" all the gluten-forming proteins and cause them to align together in such a way that they become long, elastic strands. Remember when we compared the endosperm (gluten) to an egg white? Egg whites beaten vigorously will form meringue, which makes a sort of shell when baked. That's exactly what happens when gluten is kneaded, it forms a "shell" for the bread.

But how much kneading is required? Aha, there's the burning question! Often, an otherwise successful recipe is ruined by under kneading, especially when the kneading is done by hand. This is why I'm so partial to kneading by machine; it gets the job done faster and with much less effort.

Oh, but I can already hear you thinking, "What about those recipes for no-knead bread? How do they work?" All right, you caught me. The other way to form gluten is to add time instead of kneading. No-knead recipes typically have a long resting period, often left overnight in the fridge. During the mixing stage, enough agitation takes place that, when left alone for several hours, the gluten can still form. Often you will still knead the dough just a tiny bit, a few easy turns to bring it all together. But hold on. Before you decide to park your dough in the fridge and skip the kneading step altogether, another difference is in the recipe. A no-knead recipe uses a lot more liquid; it's practically a batter bread. It works great for white flour, but leaving whole grain dough for several hours produces a sour flavor, and not a good one, like with real sourdough bread. If you want to skip kneading, then you'll have to get a different book, because it won't work with my method.

Well, that was a fun little rabbit trail we got sidetracked on. Back to how much time you should spend kneading. In the next section, I'll give you a little test you can perform on the dough at any stage of kneading, whether you're using a machine or your own two hands, that will tell you exactly whether you have kneaded enough or not. It's called a gluten window, or windowpane test, and it's been used by professional bakers for ages to determine the perfect amount of kneading for a successful loaf of bread.

---

### Action Steps

Do you have all the ingredients you need to make bread?

____Fresh Flour

____Vegetable Oil

____Sea Salt or Realsalt®

____Vital Wheat Gluten

____Rolled Oats

____Honey, ECJ, or Sucanat

____Instant Yeast

____Dough Enhancer® or equivalent

No More Bricks!

Four Brickbuster Secrets

How to Make Bread in Ten Easy Steps

Machine-Specific Directions

Spiral Mixer

Stand Mixer

Food Processor

Bread Machine

Hand Method

No More Bricks!

## Brickbuster Secrets

Now that we have our tools and ingredients, we're ready to get started baking! One of the brickbuster secrets we've already talked about - do you remember? It's making sure you use hard wheat, spelt, or kamut as your base flour.

There are four more secrets you need to learn. Some of these may be new to you, canceling out long-held beliefs about how bread should be made. But I'll explain each one so that you understand why it's done this way.

- Use HOT water

- Never measure the flour

- Test for gluten development

- Handle finished dough with oil only, not flour

### 1. Use Hot Water

Typically every bread recipe in the world begins by instructing you to measure the temperature of water to 105-110°. Many people skip this step of measuring the temperature, and either end up with water that is too cool for the yeast to activate, or so hot that it kills the yeast.

The problem with using warm water, is that it will not stay warm. As soon as it's poured into the bowl, some of the heat begins to be absorbed by the bowl itself. As more ingredients are added, they too, will begin to absorb some of the heat from the water, resulting in liquid that has lost several degrees in temperature. So starting out with hot water ensures that there is enough heat to warm the bowl and the other ingredients. Hot water makes warm dough, and warm dough creates the perfect environment for yeast to thrive.

How hot is hot? The hottest water that comes out of your faucet. Assuming that you don't burn yourself in the shower, your hot water heater is probably set to a safe temperature of 120° to 125°. If you use bottled water and need to heat it, you'll have to use a thermometer, so that you're sure it's not above 130°, or you risk killing your yeast.

Remember that, in our quick & easy method, we will not take time to dissolve or even moisten the yeast directly in the water. It will be added last, on top of all the other dry ingredients.

### 2. Never Measure the Flour

The real key of this step is that you should learn to make bread by "feel." This is, of course, a very subjective process, and is easier to do when mixing by machine than by hand. What I mean by not measuring is that you should not automatically dump in all the flour that is called for in a recipe, because most bread recipes use about 15 to 20% too much flour. When too much flour is added, the bread is dense, dry, and crumbly. By simply decreasing the amount of flour you are currently using in your recipes, you may likely have lighter, softer, moister bread. While it is perfectly fine to measure and set aside the amount specified, do not feel that you need to actually use all of it or that you cannot add more if needed. Also, do not assume that it will be exactly the same amount next time you make bread.

Methods for measuring flour in cups (by volume instead of weight) affect the amount of flour that ends up in the dough. For example, when "scooping" the flour into the cup, it becomes more densely packed, and thus contains more flour. On the other hand, sifting or spooning flour into the cup adds air, resulting in less flour going into the cup. This can significantly affect the outcome of the bread. Other factors affecting the amount of flour used include the texture (how finely or coarsely it was ground) and regional weather variances. Since you can't possibly know any of the recipe author's variables, there must be some give and take when it comes to adding flour.

So, how to tell? This will be covered in more detail later, but when mixing by machine, the dough will form a ball in the middle, sticking to itself instead of the sides and bottom of the machine. When the dough ball cleans the interior of the bowl, and there is little or no sticky residue remaining, this is a good indication that the amount of flour is just right. It should still be a little sticky, or tacky.

## 3. Test for Gluten Development

After mixing the dough, the next step is kneading. This is the part where most recipes tell you to "continue kneading until dough becomes smooth and elastic." But how much is enough? And can you knead too much, especially if using a machine? So that you will never have to wonder about this again, here's the trick I mentioned earlier. To find out when it's okay to stop kneading, you'll perform the "gluten window" test.

Pinch off a walnut-sized piece of dough and roll it in your hands to form a ball. Now flatten the ball into a disc shape, and gently begin stretching and pulling it outward. Think back to when you were a kid with a wad of bubble gum in your mouth, preparing to blow a bubble. You worked the piece of gum in your mouth, flattening and smoothing it out so it would stretch thin and make a monster bubble. This is how your piece of dough should look and feel in your hands. If it doesn't stretch easily, or it breaks and tears right away, then more kneading time is required. In fact, it's actually a good thing to do a test window when you know it will fail. It gives you a point of reference for seeing how the dough steadily improves with more kneading. Replace the dough ball into your bowl, and continue kneading for a time. Repeat the process of pinching off a piece and try the test

again. Raise it just slightly above your head, toward the light. The goal is to have a little "window" that is translucent – allowing light to be visible through the thin membrane of dough. If it is translucent, congratulations! You have successfully kneaded the dough for the proper amount of time to have adequate gluten formation. This is especially good news for those of you purists out there who prefer to hand knead. You can always know for certain when it's okay to stop!

## 4. Handle with Oil Only

You'll have to forget grandmotherly images of flour flying through the air as it's sprinkled liberally all over the dough and counter top. Instead, you will lightly oil your hands and any surface that the dough will touch. I try to do my mixing in a separate place from my dividing and shaping, just for this reason. Any part of the dough that comes into contact with flour at this point will create a weak spot in the dough. This is because the newly-added flour hasn't had its gluten developed.

## How to Make Bread in Ten Quick & Easy Steps

Here's an overview of how to make bread the No More Bricks Quick & Easy way:

1. Mill Fresh Flour
2. Measure Ingredients
3. Mix
4. Knead
5. Divide & Deflate
6. Shape
7. Rise
8. Bake
9. Cool
10. Slice, Store, or Freeze

These directions are stated in general terms and apply to most mixers, but you should consult the specific instructions for your mixer or machine before attempting your first recipe, as there will be slight differences in each.

### Step One: Mill Fresh Flour

Put grain in your mill and turn it on. While this is running, you can start Step Two. If you're using cold or frozen flour, it's better to take it out in advance to let it warm up a little. You can still use it cold, but it will take your bread longer to rise.

lowed by the remaining dry ingredients, except the flour and yeast. Put each ingredient aside, so you know you've already used it. (Can you tell I've had trouble in this department before?) Add about half the recommended flour, making a "blanket" that will cover the water. Finally, evenly sprinkle the yeast on top.

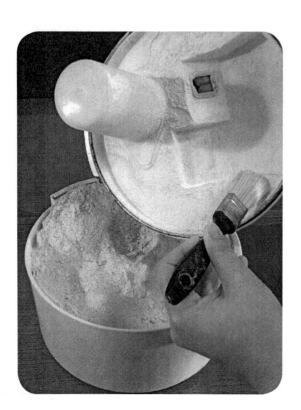

## Step Two: Measure Ingredients

Make sure you get out all the ingredients that will go into your dough, so you don't accidentally leave any out. Also get ready any add-ins that you'll use after the dough is mixed. Pre-measure all of the ingredients first, or dump them in as you go. Pour the liquids in first, fol-

## Step Three: Mix

First, it's important to note the distinction between mixing and kneading. Mixing implies that ingredients are still being added, or are not yet fully blended. The goals in mixing bread dough are to:

No More Bricks!

Completely incorporate the yeast into the mixture

Attain the proper liquid-to-flour ratio

Once you've done this, you will be ready to officially start kneading. Using a machine makes it easy to tell where the mixing ends and the kneading starts. By hand method, it's harder, because the only way to finish adding the flour (mixing) is to start kneading. That makes the kneading seem twice as long!

It may seem like I'm overstating a simple point here, but you'll understand why in a few minutes.

To begin mixing, gently pulse or mix at low speed until the flour is moistened. Increase speed and begin adding flour a little at a time. Continue adding flour slowly, and when you hear the mixer "gear down" from the extra volume in the bowl, turn up the speed. Always watch the bottom and sides of the bowl. If the dough is very wet and still sticking to the bottom, more flour is required. If it's dry and crumbly, you have already added too much flour, and now you'll have to add more water. It's easier to correct a wet dough than a dry dough, so watch carefully and try not to add too much flour too soon. Whole wheat flour absorbs liquid more slowly than white flour does, so allow a little bit more time in between additions the closer you get to the end. You're looking for dough that clings to itself and forms a ball that cleans the sides and bottom of the bowl. You may see the dough form a ball, then a few seconds later, collapse and stick to the sides again. This is because the flour is continually absorbing more liquid. I can't say this enough: do not add too much flour! The dough should still be a little tacky.

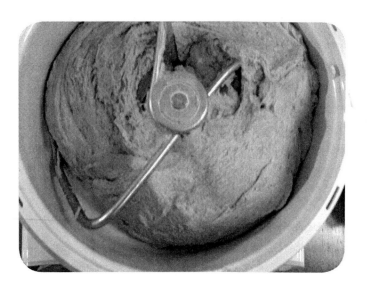

## Step Four: Kneading

Kneading is the working of the dough to develop gluten, without which your bread may rise and then fall into a brick. Do not begin the timing of the kneading until after the last of the flour has been mixed in. Technically, there is some kneading going on during the mixing. But the reason for the official delineation is so that every last grain of flour gets its gluten developed. In other words, if you decide your dough is still a little too sticky toward the end of kneading and then add some more flour, well then, the flour you just added will not have proper gluten activation. It could result in a weak spot in the dough, creating dense, doughy pockets in the baked bread. This is one reason for Brick-buster Secret #4 – don't add any more flour to "finished" dough.

The amount of kneading time will vary widely according to your mixer or machine (or bless you, your hands). Once you're familiar with how long your machine takes, set a timer for kneading, but do not walk away and leave the machine unattended while it is kneading. With mixers, the dough will sometimes "walk" up the dough hook and collect on top, where centrifugal force may cause it to fling across the room! Keep a spatula handy for this purpose. Stop the machine and scrape down the dough a little if needed. Never put your fingers or any tool inside the bowl (even just the edges) while it is running. Also, some machines will vibrate and move around a little bit on the counter. When the timer goes off, check your dough for adequate gluten development by performing the gluten window test.

Food Processors: Take care not to overknead the dough when using a food processor. Because of its intense speed, it can easily overwork the gluten strands, causing them to "break" and have the appearance of tiny, short strands in the dough instead of long, stringy ones. The dough will seem heavy and unyielding instead of springy and flexible.

Hand Kneading: No worries about overkneading here! Your arms will fall off from exhaustion long before the dough is overworked. The difficulty is in making sure you knead enough. Use a light, rhythmic motion, and do not press hard, pushing the dough into the counter. Doing so will spread the dough out into a thinner layer, exposing more surface area and requiring more flour to keep it from sticking. You need to use a light touch, constantly folding and refolding, rocking back and forth. Remember, it's not pressure; it's constant, rhythmic motion that does the trick. Use a bench knife, when need-

ed, to scrape the dough off the counter from the bottom, folding it back over onto itself and patting the wet spots with a little flour. Keep the dough mounded up on itself as much as possible, in a fairly bulky package, until it begins to hold its own shape. Perform the gluten window test as often as you like, to make sure you don't knead a single second longer than you have to!

## Step Five: Dividing & Deflating

Now that you've gotten a successful gluten window, make sure that no more flour comes into contact with the dough, and that your hands and work surface are lightly oiled. Use a bowl scraper to easily get all of the dough out of the bowl, then use your bench knife to cut the dough into the desired number of portions. The fewer times you cut into the dough at this point, the better, because the gluten strands do not "heal" once they've been cut.

My recipes are designed to be divided into 1½ pound portions. If you have more than one loaf, I think it's best to weigh each one so that they'll bake at the same rate, but you may prefer to eyeball the amounts to save time. Each 1½ pounds of dough will make the following:

- 1-2 pizza crusts

- 4 soup bowls

- 8 hamburger/hot dog buns

- 8-12 cinnamon rolls

- 12-16 dinner rolls

Before shaping each loaf, the excess air needs to be removed. In just the last couple minutes of dividing, the yeast has already begun to do its work, and the dough will almost immediately begin to appear puffy.

You can deflate the dough in one of two ways: roll each piece out with a rolling pin, or pick up each piece and throw it down hard on the counter several times. The latter is my preferred method, because it's quick and a lot more fun! Since I don't have to knead by hand, this is how I get my stress relief. Don't be afraid of hurting the dough; remember it has already been stretched and pulled quite a lot during the kneading process. Whenever the dough begins to stick to your hands or the counter, spritz on a little more oil.

## Step Six: Shaping

To form a loaf, there are three steps: stretch, tuck, and pinch. Begin by pulling the dough outward from the center with both hands at the same time, then tuck the edges underneath on both sides. This helps the dough to rise more evenly and have a beautifully round top. Place the dough topside down on the counter, and pinch the side and end edges together to seal. Holding onto this seam, rock the dough back and forth a bit to smooth the top a bit. Pick it right-side up again and you should have a tapered oval or football shape. Smooth out any dents, if needed, nest it into an oiled pan, and cover it with a tightly woven cloth. Spritz the towel with a little water for added moisture. Set a timer, so you and your bread can both take a nice little power nap.

## Shaping Rolls or Buns

The natural inclination here is to just roll the dough into a ball in your hands, like play dough. If you do this, it will have random seams and creases that will cause it to rise unevenly. If you're in a hurry and don't mind a "rustic" looking roll, no problem. If you want perfectly round, uniform shapes, use a variation of the stretch-tuck-and-pinch method described above, but on a smaller scale. Pull each roll outward from the center and tuck the edges underneath in all directions, sort of like a balloon, with a round top and pointy bottom. Pinch the bottom closed and place them on a greased or parchment paper-lined baking sheet, or in greased muffin tins. Flatten each one slightly with your fingers if you want it to have a gentle dome, rather than be a tall bowling ball shape.

## Panning

I never gave much thought to the type of pan I used in baking, assuming that one loaf pan or cookie sheet was as good as another. But this isn't so! If you haven't done so already, make sure to read about choosing baking pans in Chapter 3.

## Greasing Pans

Be sure to grease your pans well so that the bread is easier to remove from the pan. You will probably still have to use a knife to help loosen the baked loaves unless you add a little liquid lecithin to your oil. This causes bread to slide effortlessly right out of the pan. See more info on preparing an oil-lecithin mixture, as well as cleaning and storing pans in the Tips chapter. You can also use a commercial nonstick spray, but I prefer not to because of additional chemi-

cal propellants they use in them. The overspray often stains the pans and won't come off.

## Step Seven: Rising

The purpose of raising dough is to allow the yeast time to reproduce, doing its work of making the dough expand to light and feathery heights. During this time it will also develop flavor in the bread. The longer and slower the rise, the better the flavor and texture will be. Another benefit of allowing the dough to rise, or rest, is to allow the gluten strands to relax, making the dough easier to handle and shape.

## Single Rise

For the speediest bread possible, allow just one rise, after shaping. Since traditional methods call for more than one rise, the word "proofing" is often assigned to this specific period of rising – between shaping and baking. The time needed for this step will depend on multiple factors, discussed below.

## Location and Environment of Rising Dough

Ideally, the dough should be allowed to rise in a warm place, about the same temperature that is comfortable to you (70° – 80°), so that the temperature of the dough remains warm enough for yeast action to continue. It should be free of drafts, especially cool drafts, to keep it from drying out or shrinking. Covering with a lightweight, slightly damp towel will also protect the dough from drying out and forming a "skin" which could lead to a crust that separates from the bread during baking.

During the first ten or so minutes of baking, the dough will continue to rise. This is called oven spring, and it must be taken into account when deciding how long to allow the dough to rise before being placed into the oven.

A rule of thumb for loaves baked in pans (as opposed to free-form shapes) is to watch for the center of the loaf (the dome) to rise to one inch above the sides of the pan. Remember that the volume of dough you use must be appropriate to the size of your pan, or this guideline will lead you astray. If you have too large a pan, the dough will not rise to that level because it will expand sideways more and upward less. Conversely, if the dough rises to the point that it is spilling over and drooping down the outer sides of the pan in a mushroom shape, it has risen too much. It must then be taken out, deflated, reshaped, and allowed to rise again

Some people advise placing dough in the oven, which is either cold or has been turned on for a short time to warm the interior. I personally prefer not to raise my bread in the oven. It would be very easy to either forget the dough is in there and let it rise too long, or else run the risk of having the oven be too warm and the dough rise too fast. Bread that is raised too quickly or in too warm a place often has an overly yeasty flavor. Also, what to do when the bread is finished rising and it's time to preheat the oven?

If the dough is still warm (as it should be, if you started out with hot water), then allowing it to rise on the table or counter top is usually sufficient. Sometimes if I have started out with cold or frozen flour and my dough isn't as warm as it should be, I'll place it next to the oven, which is turned on to begin preheating. I never place it ON the oven, as the bottom of the pan can conduct too much heat to the dough.

## Factors Affecting Rising times

- Amount of yeast in the recipe: More yeast = faster, higher rise

- Temperature of the dough

- Temperature of the room

- Humidity

## Terms Related to Raising Dough

Here are some terms that you may come across in recipes and cookbooks. They all basically mean allowing the dough to rest, but have different names according to what stage the bread is in. If you'd like to know more about slowing down your breadmaking (thereby making practical use of the following terms), see the Tips chapter.

Fermentation – the first and second rising before dough is shaped; also refers to the chemical process of yeast as it reproduces.

Autolyse (AUTO-leeze) – a resting stage of the dough between mixing and kneading, to allow the flour to fully absorb the liquid

Proofing (of dough) – refers to the final stage of rising, after shaping. Don't confuse this with proofing of yeast, which refers to the dissolving of active dry yeast prior to mixing it into the dough

Ripeness – quality of a dough that has fully fermented, often tested by inserting two fingers into the dough: if the impression fills or springs back, it is not ripe; if the impression remains intact, the dough is ripe. You won't need to perform this test using the quick & easy method.

Oven Spring – the rising that takes place during the first 10 minutes of baking.

After the bread has risen, you may like to garnish your bread by either glazing, scoring, or sprinkling with some seeds. This is an optional step; you may proceed directly to baking at this point.

## Finishing Touches

This is probably the easiest and most enjoyable way to personalize your bread and show your creative side. Use your own unique marking system to distinguish one flavor of bread from another or simply decorate your bread to suit your mood.

### Glazing

Glazing adds shine and/or color to the crust. Using different liquids will produce a variety of results, from a shiny to dull finish, with varying degrees of color contrast. Glazing can also act like a glue to stick seeds or other decorations to the crust. Some glazes should be applied before baking, while others can be applied before or after baking.

**Before Baking:**

- Water
- Egg Wash
- Milk
- Oil
- Butter

**During Baking:**

- Water (every 10 min)

**After Baking**

- Shortening
- Butter
- Olive Oil
- Water

Brushing or misting with water will create a crunchy, chewy crust, similar to that of French bread. Since it quickly either absorbs or evaporates, it must be repeated in frequent intervals. Moisten the crust after rising, just before placing into the oven. Use a water spray bottle to spray additional water on the crust every five to ten minutes during baking. Do this very quickly, so you can close the oven door and keep the heat inside. Placing a pan of ice cubes or water on the bottom rack of the oven will create even more steam inside the oven, which will also contribute to a crispy crust.

### Egg Wash

This creates a shiny, glossy crust with a just-came-from-the-bakery look. The concentration of egg yolk and/or milk fat will cause varying tints of golden yellow. For shine without color, use egg white and water alone.

With one tablespoon of water, milk, or cream, beat your choice of the following: One whole egg, one egg yolk, or one egg white.

## Milk

Brush lightly with any type of milk: whole, low-fat, or skim. The sugars in the milk will caramelize, browning the crust and adding flavor.

## Oil or Shortening

Brush lightly with oil of choice or shortening. I prefer not to glaze with oil before baking, as it leaves a cloudy film on the bread.

## Scoring or Slashing

Aside from decoration, scoring the dough has a purpose, especially for larger free-form loaves (baguettes or round loaves baked without a pan): it provides a controlled opening for the steam to escape. Without it, the pressure of steam building up inside the baking bread can cause a crack or "blowout" in the spot of least resistance, possibly resulting in a lopsided or misshapen appearance.

For loaves that are baked in pans, this step is less necessary, as the shape of the pan will always cause the loaves to crack just under the crest (the curved edge on either long side) of the loaf on one side.

Scoring is best done immediately before baking, after the final rise. Make quick cuts with a sharp razor blade or serrated knife, and cut at an angle, not straight up and down, for the best "opening" effect.

Some popular patterns are:

- three diagonal slashes
- tic-tac-toe design
- an X or cross
- star – four or five slashes outward from the center
- straight line down the middle

## Garnishing

A sprinkling of various seeds, rolled or finely-cracked grains, cheese, or herbs can give an attractive look to breads, and also serves to help identify any special ingredients found within. For example, I enjoy adding a few rolled oats to the top of my oatmeal bread and jalapeños to the top of my Jalapeño Jack bread. A few rings of red onion, bell peppers, or sliced olives arranged randomly or in a pretty pattern on large free-form loaves is very festive. Add cheese in the last few minutes of baking so it doesn't turn too dark.

Dusting or stenciling with flour adds an artsy, rustic, "old world" look to breads. To stencil a design, use a premade stencil or make your own from parchment paper. Hold it over your bread and sift flour through a sieve into the open design. Remove it carefully, so you don't spill any extra flour from the paper and mar the design.

## Step Eight: Baking

Here's a news flash: all ovens are different. No matter what brand or type, they all seem to have their own personality. That's why I provide a range of baking times on my recipes. I am always a little nervous when I have to use an "unknown" oven for the first time at a new class location. There just is no predicting exactly how long it will take to bake. The oven's size, age, type (convention or convection, gas or electric), amount of residual food splatters, and amount of items baked at one time can all affect the length of time required for baking. The use of an oven thermometer will help you to determine if your oven is actually operating at the temperature to which it is set.

## Loading the Oven

Since I do all of my breadmaking in large batches, knowing how much I can put into the oven at one time is of crucial importance. Not only do I want to save time in the kitchen, but energy costs are a factor as well, especially in the summer when the oven and the air conditioner are at war with each other. Furthermore, the timing of baking cycles can affect other items waiting to be baked, potentially causing overrising.

For most conventional ovens, I recommend using only one rack of the oven at a time to bake loaves of bread. Since these do not distribute heat as evenly as convection ovens, some additional "margins" are needed around the food, to prevent the heat from being trapped in one spot. On the other hand, for dinner rolls or any shape that results in a smaller mass of dough, it may be possible to achieve adequate baking on dual shelves, if the pans are rotated. Just be aware that every time the door is opened, a loss of heat will occur.

To determine the most efficient use of space in your oven, measure the length and width of one of the oven racks. Do not remove it to measure it, because you will need to take into account any protrusions in between the racks (such as the supporting tracks) that would lessen the

No More Bricks!

amount of usable space. Next, measure the baking pans that you have available, or simply arrange them on the oven rack to fit, without overcrowding. Make sure there is some space in between each pan, at least one inch, to allow for heat circulation. Try several combinations with different types of pans. Knowing this will help you in deciding how many of one particular shape of bread your oven can hold. If you have room for a larger sheet pan, or more loaf pans, then purchasing these will help you to get the maximum energy benefit from your oven. For example, in my own oven, I can easily fit six to eight loaf pans at one time, OR two sheet pans, OR one sheet pan and three loaf pans, OR one pizza pan and three loaf pans. You may want to draw simple diagrams of these arrangements and tape them to the inside of a kitchen cabinet door for future reference, to remind yourself of the most efficient use of dough and baking space.

As mentioned earlier, the first stage of baking is called oven spring. The bread rises or "springs" up very quickly at this point because the higher temperature causes rapid yeast activity. Once the internal temperature of the bread reaches 140º, the yeast can no longer survive and dies. This is also the point at which the bread will begin to fall, if it has not had sufficient gluten development. The gluten provides the structure needed to hold up the weight of the bread after the air pressure from the action of the yeast has ceased.

Make sure the oven is preheated, and once the bread is inside, try not to open the door for at least the first half of the baking time. Opening the oven door releases heat, and reduces the temperature by as much as 25º or 50º. Constant heat is required for even baking. If your oven has "hot spots" or the bread tends to brown on one side more than another, then turn the bread halfway through baking for even browning.

If your bread browns excessively, bordering on the burned side before it is done, you may need to apply an aluminum foil tent during the last few minutes of baking. This will allow the inside of the bread to keep baking, while directing some of the heat away from the crust. To do this, fold a piece of aluminum foil (shiny side facing away from the bread, to reflect heat) in half, making a tent or roof over the bread. There should be plenty of air flowing in between the foil and the bread, so make sure the foil is not wrapped tightly. If the steam cannot escape, the crust will become soggy.

## How To Tell When Bread Is Done

Three tests exist for determining whether bread is fully baked: the color of the crust, a hollow sound when tapping on the bottom, and the internal temperature. The first two are somewhat subjective, and will require some experience in order to interpret them correctly. The last test, checking for temperature, is virtually fool-proof.

When using an unfamiliar oven or a new recipe, begin to check on your bread a couple of minutes before the end of the prescribed baking time. Do not assume that because the crust is brown, the bread is done. The color of the crust will vary depending on the amount of fat and sugar in the dough, the glazing applied, if any, as well as the type of pan being used. I learned this the hard way once, when I took some bread out of the pan too soon. Although appearing golden brown, the crust was not yet set, and the sides collapsed inwardly from my grasp. I immediately replaced the bread to the oven to continue baking, but the dents remained to mar my otherwise beautiful loaf.

The "tapping" or "thumping" test can also be misleading. This requires removing the bread from the pan, turning it upside down, and tapping on the bottom to see if it sounds hollow. Using this method, I have also been disappointed. Once, upon hearing what I assumed to be a successful hollow thump, I left my bread to cool. When slicing into it later, I found a small doughy section in the middle, too late to return to the oven for more baking.

I think the safest and most accurate way to test for doneness is to use an instant-read thermometer. Plunge it into the center of the bread, and if it reads 190°, the bread is done, without question. If you do not want to make a hole in the top of the bread, you can insert it in an existing air hole or crack, or on one long side, just under the crest of the loaf. Make sure it goes to the exact center of the bread, since that is the last place to complete baking. Do not insert the thermometer from the short end of the loaf, or every slice will have a hole in it!

The only time this test is not quite accurate is when there is filling rolled up inside the bread. If the thermometer comes into contact with any filling that's high in sugar or fat, it will cause a higher reading on the thermometer than the surrounding bread. Filled breads often need to bake a few minutes longer than those that aren't filled, due to the extra moisture and steam inside.

Beep! Beep! Beep! Joy of joys, the bread is done! Herein lies one more benefit of making

bread in bulk: you can eat a whole loaf fresh from the oven, and still have more bread leftover for the next day, as well as some to freeze and some to give away!

## Step Nine: Cooling

Remove loaves from their pans immediately onto cooling racks so they do not become soggy. Putting them to rest on their sides will provide a little more air circulation at the bottom of the loaf, where it's most needed. Rolls should be slid off of their pans, via parchment paper, onto a cooling rack. Then pull out the parchment paper from under them, in the manner of a magician's tablecloth trick.

Now comes the hardest part: you must wait at least 15 minutes before attempting to slice and eat your bread! Set the timer and your resolve to not pinch off little mouse bites. Perhaps knowing the reasoning behind this rule will help to fortify your self-discipline.

Bread that is fresh from the oven is, thanks to our friend yeast and his bubbles, full of tiny little air pockets. These pockets are now full of moisture, which, when cut, will soak into the surrounding bread, making it soggy and difficult to slice evenly, as well as deflating the entire loaf. Postponing the slicing allows the moisture time to evaporate, and gives the interior of the loaf time to solidify. At the same time, the formation of the crust crust is still in progress, as the carmelization of the sugars in it continues to impart flavor into the moist interior. Besides, you cannot appreciate the taste of overly hot food anyway, so the pleasure of eating is enhanced all around by this short delay.

If you plan to package your bread for storage or freezing, you'll need to let it cool completely, anywhere from three to five hours, depending on the size and shape of the bread.

## Step Ten: Slicing, Storing, and Freezing

The longer the bread cools, the easier it is to slice. A serrated knife ensures straight, even slicing. If you prefer thin slices for sandwiches or toast, an electric knife is the perfect tool for the job. Either way, I find it's easier to slice bread by laying it on its side, rather than cutting down through the top. Wooden or plastic bread slicing guides – rectangular "garages" that house a loaf of bread and have evenly-spaced slots for the knife to be inserted through – can also help make even slices.

The crust acts as a barrier to keep the inside of the bread, known as the crumb, fresh and

moist. Once it is sliced open, air can permeate the entire loaf through the cut side. I prefer to cut slices as I use them, instead of slicing the entire loaf. The more exposure to air there is, the more quickly the bread will go stale.

Bread must be completely cooled before packaging, or the remaining steam will be trapped as moisture inside the bag or container, causing sogginess and inviting mold. If you must wrap a still-warm loaf, put it inside a paper lunch bag, which is porous enough to allow some heat and moisture to escape.

Never store bread in the refrigerator – it will dry out many times faster than leaving it at room temperature. In fact, it's been said that a day in the refrigerator is equal to six days on the shelf! I store my bread in plastic bread bags, removing as much air from them as possible before clipping shut. Some people feel that leaving bread to "breathe" in a bread box instead of trapping it in an airtight container maintains the flavor and keeps the crust from becoming too soft. This is a personal preference and will largely depend on how soon you plan to finish off your bread. Also consider whether visitors of the six-legged variety might be attracted to it.

Using these recipes and techniques, your bread should remain soft and fresh for the first three to four days. Around the fourth or fifth day, it begins to dry out, and is better to use for toast, French toast, or grilled sandwiches. If you haven't used it all within five to six days, cut it into cubes or crumble it into bread crumbs, and store those in a plastic bag in the freezer to keep them from molding. These can then be used for stuffing, croutons, breakfast casseroles, bread pudding, crumb topping for casseroles, or crumb coatings for meats. I have even used an ultra-frugal recipe for cookies that substitutes bread crumbs for the flour!

If you do not intend to consume your bread within two to three days, freeze it right away to preserve optimal freshness. Wrap it in foil and/or place it in a freezer storage bag. Remove as much air as possible from the bag by closing it most of the way and inserting a drinking straw in the open corner. Gently draw the air out through the straw, creating a vacuum and causing a shrink-wrap effect. Be careful not to exert too much pressure and collapse the bread. More freezing information can be found in the Tips chapter.

## Spiral Mixer Method

1. Mill fresh flour. If you've frozen flour previously, take it out to warm up prior to mixing bread.

2. Measure liquids into the mixing bowl. Add remaining ingredients except flour and yeast. Add about half the recommended amount of flour, followed by the instant yeast on top.

3. Mix at speed 1 until a batter is formed. Gradually add flour while mixing, turning up to speed 2 or 3 as the dough gets heavier. Add flour just until the dough begins to pull away from the sides and bottom of the bowl. Do not add too much flour; the dough should be a little sticky to the touch.

4. After the last of the flour has been added, begin the timing of the kneading, about four to six minutes at speed 2 or 3.

5. Remove dough from bowl with greased hands. On a lightly greased surface, divide dough into desired portions, using a bench knife or serrated knife to cut, and a scale to weigh each portion. Remove excess air by slamming each piece about six times on a greased surface.

6. Form dough into loaves or other desired shapes. Use the stretch-tuck-and-pinch method for even rising. Place dough in greased pans.

7. Cover and allow dough to rise to one inch above the pan for loaves, or until doubled in size for other shapes.

8. Bake at 350° until internal temperature reaches 190°.

9. Remove from pans immediately and allow to cool on racks for fifteen minutes before slicing, three to five hours before packaging.

10. Slice, store, or freeze.

## Stand Mixer Method

**Warning:** Check your specific mixer's instructions for the maximum amount of whole grain flour it can mix.

1. Mill fresh flour. If you've frozen flour previously, take it out to warm up prior to mixing bread.

2. Measure liquids into the mixing bowl. Add remaining ingredients except flour and yeast. Add about half the recommended amount of flour, followed by the instant yeast on top. Attach the mixing paddle to the mixer.

3. Mix on low speed until the flour is moistened, continue mixing at a higher speed until the mixture forms a batter. While mixing, gradually add flour, turning up the mixer speed when the motor begins to labor. Allow each addition of flour to incorporate before adding more. Add flour only until the dough cleans the sides and bottom of the bowl and sticks to itself in a large, tacky ball.

4. Replace the paddle with the dough hook, and knead. If the dough "walks" up the dough hook, stop the machine and scrape it down with a spatula. Perform the gluten window test; continue kneading if necessary.

5. Remove dough from bowl with bowl scraper and greased hands. On a lightly-greased

surface, divide dough and weigh it into loaf portions. Remove excess air by slamming each piece about six times on the counter, or roll the dough flat with a rolling pin.

6. Form into loaves or other desired shapes. Use the stretch-tuck-and-pinch method for even rising. Place dough in greased pan(s).

7. Allow to rise to one inch above the pan for loaves, or until doubled in size for other shapes.

8. Bake at 350° degrees until internal temperature reaches 190°.

9. Remove from pan(s) immediately and allow to cool on rack(s) for fifteen minutes before slicing, three-five hours before packaging.

10. Slice, store, or freeze.

## Food Processor Method

**Warning:** Check your specific machine's instructions for the maximum amount of whole grain flour it can process.

Note: Usually the manufacturer's instructions will tell you to put the dry ingredients in first, then add the liquids through the feed tube. I find it's a little harder to control this way, so if you have trouble, you may prefer to reverse this order and add flour to the liquids instead.

1. Mill fresh flour. If you've frozen flour previously, take it out to warm up prior to mixing bread.

2. If your machine has one, use the plastic blade, which is preferable to the metal blade for bread dough. Add the instant yeast to the bottom of the bowl, followed by the flour, remaining dry ingredients, and oil.

3. Because the processor generates a lot of heat, you may need to use warm water, about 105°-110°, instead of hot water. (If you're not sure if your processor is making

the dough too hot, use your thermometer to check the temperature of the dough at any point.) After locking the lid in place, use the pulse switch while gradually, sl-o-o-owly adding water through the feeder tube. Pause the machine frequently for several seconds to allow the flour time to absorb the water, since whole wheat flour takes longer to absorb liquid than white flour. You may not need all of the water. Watch the bottom of the bowl: if the mixture is still dry, add a small amount of water; if it is too wet, add a little flour. The dough is just right when it pulls away from the sides and bottom of the bowl, and forms a ball that rides around on the blade. Note: Sweet doughs (those rich in eggs, sugar, milk, and/or butter) will not clean the inside of the bowl as well as a traditional dough.

4. Turn the machine on and knead for 30-90 seconds, according to your machine's instructions. Be careful, kneading takes place VERY fast, and it's easy to overknead. (If the dough is overworked, it will again appear to be sticky, as if it needs more flour. But adding more flour at this point will not help; it will just make a stiff, heavy dough, so you'll have to start over). Perform the gluten window test; if necessary, continue to pulse the dough in the machine, a few seconds at a time, until a translucent window can be formed.

5. Handle dough with lightly greased hands. If necessary, divide dough into desired portion(s). Remove excess air by slamming dough about six times on the counter, or roll the dough flat with a rolling pin.

6. Form into a loaf or other desired shape(s). Use the stretch-tuck-and-pinch method for even rising. Place dough in greased pan.

7. Allow to rise to one inch above the pan for a loaf, or until doubled in size for other shapes.

8. Bake at 350° until internal temperature reaches 190°.

9. Remove from pan immediately and allow to cool on a rack for fifteen minutes before slicing, three to five hours before packaging.

10. Slice, store, or freeze.

## Hand Method
## (with or without hand-held mixer)

1. Mill fresh flour. If you've frozen flour previously, take it out to warm up prior to mixing bread.

2. If using a hand-held mixer, attach the beating whisks to it. If your mixer has them, switch to the dough hooks as soon as the batter turns into a soft dough. Pour the liquids into the bowl, followed by the dry ingredients, including about half the amount of recommended flour, with the instant yeast on top.

3. Mix on low speed or stir with a spoon until the flour is moistened and a batter is formed. While mixing, gradually add flour, allowing each addition to incorporate before adding more. When the mixer or spoon can no longer move through the dough easily, turn it out onto a lightly floured board, and continue mixing by hand. Add flour only until the dough can be handled more easily, not pressing too hard into the board, or it will seem to need more flour than it does. Be careful not to add too much flour; it should begin to stick to itself in a large, tacky ball. After the last of the flour has been added, remove all excess flour.

4. Lightly oil your hands and work surface and begin the timing of the kneading, about eight

to ten minutes. Perform the gluten window test; continue kneading if necessary.

5. Divide dough into desired portions. Remove excess air by slamming each piece about six times on the counter.

6. Form into loaves or other desired shapes. Use the stretch-tuck-and-pinch method for even rising. Place in greased pans.

7. Allow to rise to one inch above the pan for loaves, or until doubled in size for other shapes.

8. Bake at 350° until internal temperature reaches 190°.

9. Remove from pan(s) immediately and allow to cool on rack(s) for fifteen minutes before slicing, three to five hours for packaging.

10. Slice, store, or freeze.

When mixing by hand, the dividing line between mixing and kneading is not as clear. t is especially easy to get carried away with too much flour because it will be a gooey mess all over your hands. Use a bench knife to help scrape the dough up off the counter and fold it back onto itself.

## Bread Machine Method

Check your specific machine's instructions for its maximum capacity of dough

### Whole Wheat Cycle

Choose this setting if you want the machine to complete the loaf of bread for you, including final rising and baking.

1. Mill fresh flour. If you've frozen flour previously, take it out to warm up prior to mixing bread.

2. Pour the liquids into the pan, followed by the dry ingredients, except for the flour and

yeast. Add about half the recommended flour, followed by the yeast on top. Start the machine, and stand by to add additional flour.

3. As the bread begins to form a batter, add flour a little at a time, allowing each addition to incorporate before adding more. Watch the bottom of the pan: if it's wet and sticky, continue adding flour until the dough pulls away from the sides and bottom of the pan and sticks to itself in a large, tacky ball. You may need to use a spatula to assist in scraping down the bowl or pushing the dry flour into the mix. If the bottom of the pan still has dry flour that won't mix in, add one teaspoon of water at a time, until it all mixes together.

4-8 Allow the machine to complete its kneading, rising, and baking cycles.

9-10 Remove the bread from the machine at once and allow it to cool for 15 minutes before slicing, three to five hours before packaging.

## Dough Cycle

Choose this setting if you want the machine to mix and knead the dough only. You will then manually shape the dough, allow it to rise, and bake it in a conventional oven.

1. Mill fresh flour.

2. Pour the liquids into the pan, followed by the dry ingredients, except for the flour and yeast. Add about half the recommended flour, followed by the yeast on top. Start the machine, and stand by to add additional flour.

3. As the bread begins to form a batter, gradually add flour, allowing each addition to incorporate before adding more. Watch the bottom of the pan: if it's wet and sticky,

continue adding flour until the dough pulls away from the sides and bottom of the pan and sticks to itself in a large, tacky ball. You may need to use a spatula to assist in scraping down the bowl or pushing the dry flour into the mix. If the bottom of the pan still has dry flour that won't mix in, add one teaspoon of water at a time, until it all mixes together.

4. Allow the machine to complete the dough cycle; remove the dough when prompted for manual shaping and baking.

5. Remove excess air by slamming the dough about six times on a greased surface.

6. Form dough into a loaf or other desired shape(s). Use the stretch-tuck-and-pinch method for even rising. Place dough in a greased pan.

7. Allow to rise to one inch above the pan if it's a loaf, or until doubled in size for other shapes.

8. Bake at 350° until internal temperature reaches 190°.

9. Remove from pan immediately and allow to cool on a rack for fifteen minutes before slicing, or three to five hours before packaging.

10. Slice, store, or freeze.

No More Bricks!

Time Savers

Freezing Bread & Dough

No More Bricks!

Buy extra sets of measuring cups and spoons, and dedicate the size you most often use to be kept inside your bread ingredient containers. This will save you time in getting out those tools, then washing and putting them away. Also, look for measuring sets that have more sizes than usual, and use the largest size spoon or cup you can to save multiple "dips" and counting errors! For example, since I almost always make six loaves of bread at a time, I store a two-tablespoon scoop (as opposed to a one-tablespoon scoop) in my dough enhancer can and another in my salt jar. I keep a ¼ cup in my yeast container and a ⅓ cup in my gluten can. It may only save a few seconds here and there, but those seconds add up into minutes in the long run! The fewer steps you have, the less of a chore it will seem.

Make up a few convenience mixes by placing the dry ingredients (except flour and yeast) into a small container or storage bag. For a six-loaf batch of my everyday whole wheat oatmeal bread, I make an assembly line and place sugar, salt, oats, gluten, and dough enhancer into each of several one-quart storage bags. It doesn't take much longer to make four or five mixes than it does one. When I'm ready to make bread, that means I only have to add four more ingredients at the time of mixing: water, oil, flour, and yeast. If you want to go ahead and add yeast to your mix, then layer the yeast on the bottom and the salt last on top, so they do not come into contact with one another. When mixing bread, add the first addition of flour first to cover the water and oil, followed by your mix. This way the yeast will pour out last, on top of all the other ingredients. If you want to add fresh flour to the mix as well, you'll have to refrigerate or freeze the whole mix, and still add a little additional flour later, since you can't know for sure how much flour to measure ahead of time.

Photocopy your most frequently used recipes, trim them down to size, and tape them inside your cabinet doors for quick reference. No digging through a recipe box or hunting through a book to find them. Use them as a checklist even if your recipes are memorized.

Form a routine for yourself when making bread. First, always start by pouring grain into your grain mill. While it runs, you have a few minutes to measure ingredients and prepare your work surface. While waiting on the kneading (but keeping a close eye on it), you can grease your pans and get out any other items needed for dividing or shaping, if you didn't already do this during flour milling. While your bread rises, clean up the counter, get out the cooling racks, and label your freezer bags, etc. As you practice, you should be able to reduce your "hands-on" work time to only 15-30 minutes, depending on your machine and the size of your batch. The more loaves you do at one time, the better your time-to-loaf ratio is.

Plan your shaping options carefully when making large batches. In general, the larger your bread shapes, the more you can bake at one time, reducing or eliminating the number of extra bake cycles (saving time and electricity). For example, if you need a lot of dinner rolls, make each one 3 ounces, instead of 1½ ounces. You can fit about the same number of larger ones on a single pan, and you won't have to make as many batches. They taste so good, people would probably have eaten two smaller rolls anyway!

Mill extra flour to keep in the freezer. Use gallon freezer bags or canisters, write the date, and be sure to label the type of flour, as most of them look exactly alike! It's best if you take frozen flour out to warm up before making bread, scooping some into a bowl so it can warm up faster. If you must use it cold, or even frozen, no biggie. Just make sure your water is hot and plan on extra time for the bread to rise.

## Freezing Bread & Dough

### Freezing Tips

I've seen a very broad range of times suggested for freezing bread, anywhere from 3 weeks to 12 months! There are two reasons for this. The first is correct packaging technique. No doubt those who are of the 3-weeks-only club aren't familiar with how to remove air from packages, which helps reduce dehydration. That's easy enough to explain to you. The second reason is personal preference. If you have a discriminating palate, you may be aware of more subtle differences in taste and texture that are above the notice of others. My opinion tends toward shorter freezing times, because I think if you have bread in the freezer for more than three months, you simply aren't eating enough of it for adequate fiber and nutritional benefits!

### Air is the Enemy!

The the most important thing to remember when freezing, aside from using freezer-rated containers and packaging, is that the less air your food comes in contact with, the better the quality will be. Even ice cubes in a freezer will eventually evaporate (sublime) so keeping food in airtight packaging is key. There are two basic ways to remove air:

- create a vacuum by suction
- displace the air with liquid or a flexible, solid substance

To create a vacuum, you can purchase one of the many vacuum sealers or "food savers" on the market. Or you can do what I do and use the poor woman's vacuum sealer: a drinking straw!

Place your food in a freezer bag, and seal it most of the way closed, leaving a ½" space open at one side. Insert a drinking straw and pinch the bag tightly around the straw to keep air from escaping. Suck out the air from the bag until it has a "shrink-wrapped" look to it. If it's a loaf of baked bread, you can easily take out too much air and smash your loaf, so stop just before the bread begins to collapse or cave in on itself.

The displacement method works with raw dough, and is described below.

## Freezing Bread & Dough

I prefer to freeze baked bread, because it's easier and thaws quickly. However, it can sometimes be convenient to have dough made up ahead of time, especially around the holidays. You can freeze it either shaped or unshaped. It's not as easy to work with dough that has been frozen, so I like to freeze it shaped, especially if it's a small shape, like a dinner roll. The problem with larger shapes, such as loaves, is that they will take longer to freeze, and will continue to rise in the middle of the dough after the outside freezes. They'll also take longer to thaw. The shorter the freezing and thawing times are, the better the quality will be.

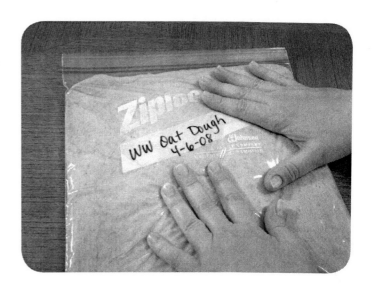

### Unshaped Dough

To freeze dough that will be shaped later, take the dough immediately after the dividing & deflating step and flatten it into a large disc shape. Coat it lightly with oil, and place it in a gallon freezer bag. Spread the dough out evenly and thinly inside the bag, so it takes up the entire space within. Push out any air bubbles and seal the top closed. You should have a thin, flat bag of dough which will both freeze and thaw very quickly. Place the dough on a tray or cookie sheet, so it stays flat, and freeze until solid. To thaw, take the dough out of the freezer and loosen or open its packaging slightly. Let it sit on the counter until it's soft enough to be pliable, then proceed with shaping and rising as usual.

### Shaped Dough

To freeze dough that's already been shaped, such as rolls or buns, place them on a greased tray or cookie sheet. Work quickly before the dough has time to rise very much, putting each one in the freezer as you go, if you have to. Cover the tray loosely with plastic wrap or foil, and put it in the freezer just until the outside of the dough is firm enough to hold its shape. Set a timer for 30 minutes to an hour, so you won't forget to take it back out again before it dries out. Once the rolls are stiff and partially frozen, put them in a freezer storage bag, and remove the air from the bag using the straw method. They should keep for two to three weeks or more.

To thaw, remove the desired number of rolls and place them, covered, on a greased cookie sheet. Depending on the size of the rolls and the temperature of the room, it will take 3-5 hours for them to thaw and rise. When they appear to have risen to nearly double their size, glaze or garnish, if desired, and bake as usual.

### Freezing Baked Bread

Make sure your bread is completely cooled, and that there is no warmth radiating from the bottom at all. Tipping baked loaves over on their sides on cooling racks can help them to cool more quickly.

Place bread in freezer storage bags, using the straw method to remove air, or you may double wrap it tightly in foil. Make sure to label the outside with a date and the type of bread, if necessary. If you prefer, you may slice the bread first, so you can remove just a few frozen slices at a time. The slices will thaw very quickly, but it may cause the loaf to dry out a little faster in the freezer.

To thaw, leave the bread in its wrapping until soft, so it can reabsorb any lost moisture. Once thawed, you may use it immediately or heat it in the oven at 350°, wrapped in foil for 10 minutes. Open the foil and continue baking for another five minutes.

## Freezing Sandwiches

Yes, Virginia, you CAN freeze sandwiches! You just need these simple techniques for assembly and packaging to keep them from getting soggy.

## Meat & Cheese

Spread both inner sides of the bread with a thin layer of margarine or softened (not melted) butter, covering the bread all the way out to the crust. This small amount of fat creates a barrier so the bread doesn't stick to the meat and become soggy. Place meat and/or cheese on one piece of buttered bread, and top with remaining slice, buttered side facing toward the filling. Be careful that you keep these cold enough after they thaw so that they do not spoil. You may need to pack other cold items or use an insulated container for this purpose.

Package several small bags or containers of lettuce leaves, pickles, or other toppings and store in the refrigerator so they'll be ready when you need them. You may even want to purchase single-serving condiment packets.

**NOTE:** Do not freeze any type of chicken or tuna salad filling that contains salad dressing or mayonnaise, since it doesn't freeze well.

## Peanut Butter & Jelly

Spread both inner sides of the bread with a layer of peanut butter, covering the bread all the way out to the crust. Spread jam or jelly on top of one peanut-buttered slice, leaving a small margin of peanut butter around it (if the jelly touches the bread, it will soak in). Top with remaining piece of bread. Leave the sandwich whole – don't cut it in half.

**To freeze:**
Wrap each sandwich in a paper towel, and place it in a sandwich bag, removing as much air as possible from the bag. Place several sandwich bags into a one-gallon freezer bag. Remove air from the larger bag by using the vacuum method described previously.

**To thaw:**
Take out individual sandwiches as needed. If you put one in your lunchbox in the morning, it should thaw by noon (keep meat & dairy products cold at all times). The paper towel absorbs extra moisture, and the way they're spread should keep them from being soggy.

## Freezing pizza, calzones, stromboli, etc.

For freezing large pizza crusts, use 2-gallon bags, 2.5 gallon "jumbo" bags, or turkey roasting bags. Since not all of these are intended for freezing, you'll need to use two or three bags layered inside each other, but they can be reused many times. Be sure to remove the excess air and you're good to go.

When freezing fully-assembled calzones and stromboli, I prefer not to include the sauce inside, as it can get soggy when thawing. Instead, freeze the sauce separately in a quart size freezer bag, store it in the larger bag with your sandwich to make a "kit," and ladle it over the top of your calzone or serve it for dipping on the side.

Pizzas and calzones should be reheated on parchment paper-lined baking sheets in a 400° oven for about 10 minutes. Calzones may need to be covered with foil on top to keep from drying out.

## Miscellaneous Tips

### Greasing Pans with Oil & Lecithin

In a condiment bottle, pour a ½" to 1" layer of liquid lecithin in the bottom. Fill the remainder with your vegetable oil of choice. Holding your finger over the spout, shake the bottle vigorously to completely mix the oil and lecithin. Once mixed, it will stay mixed. Squirt a small amount of oil mixture in the bottom and up the sides of your loaf pan, and spread it evenly with a paper towel.

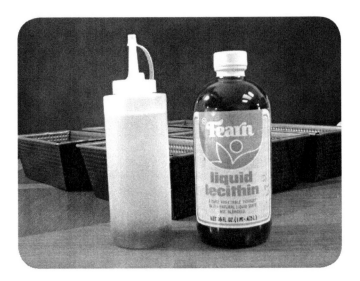

## Cleaning and Storing Pans

Because I bake often, both at home and at my classes, I seldom wash my loaf pans in between uses. This may sound shocking, but the same practice is used by many professional bakeries. Washing is hard on pans, especially automatic dishwashers, because the detergent is so harsh. My current pans are tinned steel, so they have to be handled more carefully to avoid rusting. If I have baked a gooey cinnamon-raisin bread or a pungent garlic & herb bread, then I will hand wash them, but otherwise a simple wiping out with a paper towel is usually sufficient. The slight residue of oil which is left on them helps to prevent rusting, and they will be sterilized with the next baking anyway. If you have non-stick coated pans, be careful when stacking other pans inside them, so you don't scratch them.

## Cracking Grains

If you'd like a small amount of cracked grain to add texture to your bread, place no more than ¼ cup to ½ cup of whole grains in your Bosch blender, or other good-quality blender. Pulse it until the grains are cracked to the size you want. Very large pieces of grain may damage your teeth unless softened by boiling water before adding to your bread. To knead-in cracked grains to your dough, make sure they are cracked fairly fine. The downside to this method is that you will not get perfectly uniform pieces. You'll end up with some larger and smaller pieces, as well as a fair amount of grainy dust. To remedy this, sift the cracked grain through a sieve to remove the dust.

If you'd like a lot of cracked grains for cereals, you may want to invest in a cracking mill, such as the cereal mill attachment for the Bosch blender. Most impact mills do not crack grains; the coarsest they grind is the consistency of cornmeal.

## Climate Adjustments

Climate has a huge impact on bread recipes. I live at low altitude in Missouri, where the weather is fairly humid. When I first began making bread, I had to adjust some of the recipes I was using, because they called for too much water. My mixing bowl literally overflowed when I tried to keep adding enough flour so the dough would clean the bowl. It's very likely that you will need to adjust my recipes somewhat for the area where you live, so don't feel badly if you don't get perfect bread the first few times you attempt it. Keep careful notes about what works and doesn't work, and you will improve each time.

If you live at high altitude (3000 feet or more), you have some special challenges to work out. Lower air pressure will cause your bread to rise up to 50% faster. You can compensate for this by doing all of the following:

- reduce the yeast by 25% - 50%
- reduce 1-2 tablespoons of sugar per cup called for
- raise your oven temperature by 25°

Because the air is dryer, flour will absorb very quickly. Plan to add more water to your recipe, ranging from one to four tablespoons more for every cup, depending on the level of your altitude. You may also find that it helps the texture and flavor of your bread if you allow it to rise twice instead of once.

## Slowing Down Breadmaking (on purpose or accidentally!)

You can allow your dough to rise as many as three or four times if you like, as long as you keep it moist and you have a good, strong yeast. Choose an extra rising period at any stage of the process that's most convenient for you. Sometimes this may be an unintentional

"break" when the phone is ringing off the hook or the baby is crying. Don't worry, your dough is pretty forgiving. When you come back, you should be able to proceed as if you'd never left.

**Sponging** – a sponge is a wet mixture consisting of water, yeast, flour, and sugar/honey which is allowed to rest for 30 minutes or more before the rest of the ingredients are added.

**Autolysing** – a resting period between mixing and kneading. Sometimes this stage is incorrectly referred to as sponging.

**Fermentation** – allowing the dough to rise in the bowl after kneading is complete. Cover loosely to allow for expansion, and deflate the dough when it's risen to double its original size. After deflating, allow the dough to rise again, or proceed directly to shaping.

**Proofing** – is usually the final stage of rising, just before baking. This is the only time my recipes actually call for the dough to rise. But what if that little "interruption" happens here, and the dough rises too high, spilling up and over the sides of the pan, or collapsing under its own weight? This is called overproofing, and it's no problem. Just deflate and reshape your dough, then allow it to rise again.

## Easy Clean-up

Allow the leftover bits of dough in your mixing bowl to dry. Then use a stiff dish brush to easily brush them off and throw them into the trash can. Try not to allow fresh dough to go down your drain, as it will continue to grow and can make a mess (don't ask how I know this). Allow your dividing and shaping area to dry and use a bench knife to scrape any dried bits of flour and/or oil residue before washing with a wet cloth.

The newest model of Bosch mixer has a removable center column for easy cleaning.

## Oh, No!
## What Happened to My Bread?

Once in a while, I still make a batch of bread that flops. Usually it's because I'm in a hurry and/or trying to multi-task with too many other things going on at the same time. I'll share a few of my bloopers with you as well as some common problems and solutions.

### Problem: Missing ingredient!

I have memorized my bread recipe, but occasionally I do accidentally leave out an ingredient, which is most often the salt. When I first started making bread in the Bosch mixer, I followed their directions for adding the salt last, in order to give the yeast a head start in fermenting. Either in the middle of, or at the end of kneading, it would suddenly hit me that I had left it out, so I would add the salt then and knead a little longer. During the proofing stage, I noticed the bread would tear open in little patches all over the bread, and instead of being smooth and round, it was lumpy and full of holes on top, like Swiss cheese. It came out of the oven smaller than its original size (fallen), was a little bit denser, and still lumpy-bumpy. In short, ugly bread! It still tasted okay, but it had a different texture. It took me a long time to connect the two things together. I couldn't figure out why it was beautiful one time, and ugly the next. Finally, I realized I only got ugly bread when I put the salt in late. It was the sharp edges of the grains of undissolved salt that were cutting into the gluten strands, affecting their ability to stretch.

Once I even forgot to put yeast in! I must have been deep in thought about something other than making bread, because I handled and shaped that dough without even noticing that it had no bubbles, no yeasty smell, and no lightness to it. I think you have to be a person who wears many "hats" to understand how this is possible! My body goes into auto-pilot mode, while my brain is elsewhere. It was not until 20 or 30 minutes later when I saw the same little compact loaves in the pans that I realized I had left the yeast out. Believe it or not, I was able to save that batch of bread by mixing the instant yeast with a little water, throwing the dough back in the mixer with the yeast, and remixing. I'm not sure whether that's a testimonial to the mixer, the yeast, or both. Maybe not as perfect a loaf as it otherwise would have been, but it worked out okay!

## Solution(s):

- Line up all the ingredients you need and count them. For the whole wheat oatmeal bread, there are nine ingredients. If you don't count, it can look like everything is there, when it's not.

- As you use an ingredient, put it clearly aside from the others, or put it away.

- Tape your recipe to the inside of the cabinet door, above the place where you mix bread. Use it as a checklist.

## Problem: Bread is doughy in some spots or too brown on top

## Solution(s):

- Use an oven thermometer to test the temperature of your oven in various spots. It may not be heating to the temperature for which it's been set.

- In older ovens, it's possible that you do not have even heat distribution, causing "hot spots." Try rotating the positions of the pans during baking, being careful not to keep the oven door open long. Also, try placing a baking stone or some natural clay tiles on the bottom rack and preheat these with the oven.

- Form a loose tent of aluminum foil to cover the crust, so that the bread can be baked longer without too much browning on top.

## Problem: Bread has a sour or "yeasty" taste.

## Solution(s):

- The dough is rising too quickly due to too much yeast, or it's in too warm an environment. Cut down on the yeast in your recipe, lower the water temperature, or let rise in a cooler place.

- The dough is overproofed, meaning it's risen too long.

- The bread is underbaked.

## Problem: Crust is too thick, or falls off when sliced

## Solution(s):

- Too much flour was added.

- Top of bread dried out during rising – cover loosely with plastic wrap, or a tightly-woven or damp cloth

- Bread dried out during baking – baked too long or at too low a temperature

## Problem: Bread has a large crack or hole in the side.

## Solution:

- Loaf breads typically do crack along the side underneath the crest of the loaf. If it bothers you, score the loaf on the top to allow steam to escape

- Freeform loaves need to be scored on top

## Problem: Bread is too crumbly

## Solution(s):

- Use a sharp serrated knife to slice.

- Too much or too little flour has been used.

- Gluten development was not sufficient.

## Problem: Dough does not rise well or in a reasonable time

### Solution(s):

- Use hot water to ensure warm dough. Make sure all ingredients are at room temperature or above.

- If the water is too hot, the yeast is being killed (over 130°).

- Check the yeast's expiration date or proof it to make sure it's still good.

- Add a little more yeast next time.

No More Bricks!

# PART TWO

# MASTER RECIPES & VARIATIONS

No More Bricks!

Why Master Recipes?

Whole Wheat Oatmeal Bread Master Recipe

Honey Whole Wheat Bread Master Recipe

Whole Wheat Rye Bread Master Recipe

Soft Wheat Egg Dough Master Recipe

No More Bricks!

## Why Master Recipes?

I have always enjoyed cooking and have collected tons of recipes, clipping them out of magazines, or writing them down from books. I spent a lot of time reading, sorting, and organizing them. Trouble is, once they were filed away, I often forgot about them and never got around to trying them! Then I discovered the magic of master recipes. A master recipe is a base recipe to which minor adjustments can be made for a variety of dishes. This really simplifies cooking and meal planning for me, because I have fewer recipes to choose from, but I don't get tired of preparing the same thing over and over again. I still like to look at new recipes to get ideas and try new things, but now I try to adapt the flavors and ingredients into a similar recipe with which I am already familiar. My need for creativity and experimentation is satisfied without as much time invested in the process.

I used to think that I could never write my own recipes, and was always amazed by people I knew who could make up new dishes and cook by "feel" or by "taste" without a specific recipe. I've never felt comfortable about guessing at measurements, without using exact measuring cups and spoons either. So for the most part, I resigned myself to cooking "by the book," following recipes precisely as written, in order to guarantee excellent results.

Somewhere along the way, I realized that I didn't have to come up with an entire recipe from scratch. I could simply use a recipe that I liked as a guide, altering the types or amounts of ingredients slightly. For many of you, this is probably a "duh" statement, but it was a new and liberating idea for me at the time! Remember I said at the beginning of this book, that bread is one part art? If you felt that might exclude you, because you aren't the creative type, never fear. How do artists learn their craft? Most of them start by copying other great artists. Once they have practiced imitating the strokes of a famous painting, they have a better idea of how to create their own.

This is exactly what I want you to do. Try out my recipes, and get used to the process of making bread. As you feel more confident in your ability, then add more of what you like, or take away some of what you don't like. All of the recipes in this book grew out of someone else's recipes, which I made their way for a while, before making changes of my own. I don't mean to imply that my recipes are master works of art in manner of da Vinci (or more appropriately, Julia Child), but they reflect my own taste (art is subjective after all!) and have been successful for me. It is my hope that they will be successful for you, and that they will be a source of inspiration for you to create your own masterpieces.

## Choosing a Master Recipe

I'm often asked which master recipe should be used for which variation. The short answer is, it really doesn't matter! Let your taste be your guide. But, as that doesn't seem to satisfy some people, I'll give you the breakdown of what I had in mind when I created the recipes.

## Whole Wheat Oatmeal & Honey Whole Wheat

These are basically the same recipe – one uses sugar, and one calls for honey. The only other difference is that the added oatmeal makes for a slightly lighter bread. You should plan to use these two interchangeably, and yes, it's perfectly okay to substitute honey in the Whole Wheat Oatmeal, and sugar in the Honey Whole Wheat! I've used both of these breads for every single variation in this book, including cinnamon rolls, doughnuts, etc.

If I had to be more specific though, I'd probably use the oatmeal version more often for

- dinner rolls

- hamburger buns

- soup bowls

- Sticky Picky (sweet versions)

The only thing to note about these two recipes is that there are certain variations for which you'll want to use half the amount of sugar/honey. That's why there's a range for those ingredients in the recipes. I like my "plain breads" sweeter, but for a chicken pot pie, the extra sweetness is not complimentary to the rest of the dish. Likewise, you may not care for extra sweetness in Jalapeño Jack bread or pizza crust (depends on the flavor of your sauce).

## Whole Wheat Rye Bread

I don't make this one as much, and I came up with it primarily for special occasions where I want to have more than one color of bread. I particularly like it for:

- Marble Rye

- Party Dip Bowls

- Reuben Stromboli/Calzone or other robust-flavored sandwiches

## Soft Wheat Egg Dough

This bread can also be used as an everyday bread. It's a complete protein and is richer in flavor due to the addition of eggs and milk. It's also a little lighter and softer in texture, due to the substitution of soft wheat for some of the hard wheat. I don't make sweet treats that often, but for special occasions, I like to use this dough for:

- Sweet Rolls

- Citrus Tea Ring

- Doughnuts

- Fruit Kuchen

No More Bricks!

# Whole Wheat Oatmeal Bread
## Master Recipe

| Yield: loaves | 1 | 2 | 3 | 6 |
|---|---|---|---|---|
| hot water | 1 cup | 2 cups | 3 cups | 6 cups |
| vegetable oil | 2 T. | ¼ cup | ⅓ cup | ⅔ cup |
| rolled oats | ⅔ cup | 1⅓ cups | 2 cups | 4 cups |
| Organic Cane Sugar (ECJ) or sugar* | 1-2 T. | 3T-⅓ cup | ¼ - ½ cup | ½ - 1 cup |
| vital wheat gluten | 1 T. | 2 T. | 3 T. | ⅓ cup |
| Dough Enhancer® | 1 tsp. | 2 tsp. | 1 T. | 2 T. |
| sea salt | 1 tsp. | 1½ tsp. | 1 T. | 2 T. |
| Freshly-milled hard wheat flour | 2-3 cups | 5-6 cups | 6-8 cups | 11-13 cups |
| Saf-instant® yeast | 1 T. | 1½ T. | 2 T. | 4 T. |

*ECJ = Evaporated Cane Juice Crystals, a less-refined sugar. Use less sugar when adding savory ingredients or for bread that's not as sweet.

1. Mill fresh flour

2. Measure ingredients into bowl, liquids first, then dry ingredients, using only half the flour and adding yeast last

3. Mix gently until the flour is moistened. Continue mixing, adding flour, until the dough cleans the sides and bottom of bowl

4. Knead according to machine - do the gluten window test

5. Divide dough into portions & Deflate

6. Shape into loaves or rolls and place in greased pan(s)

7. Let rise until doubled or 1" above pan

8. Bake at 350° ~30 minutes, until 190° internal temp

9. Cool on cooling racks

10. Slice after 15 minutes, store or freeze after 3-5 hours

# Honey Whole Wheat Bread
## Master Recipe

| Yield: loaves | 1 | 2 | 3 | 6 |
|---|---|---|---|---|
| hot water | 1 cup | 2 cups | 3 cups | 6 cups |
| vegetable oil | 2 T. | ¼ cup | ⅓ cup | ⅔ cup |
| honey* | 1-2 T. | 2 T - ¼ cup | 3 T -⅓ cup | ⅓ - ¾ cup |
| vital wheat gluten | 1 T. | 2 T. | 3 T. | ⅓ cup |
| Dough Enhancer® | 1 tsp. | 2 tsp. | 1 T. | 2 T. |
| sea salt | 1 tsp. | 1½ tsp. | 1 T. | 2 T. |
| freshly-milled hard wheat flour | 3-4 cups | 6-7 cups | 8-10 cups | 15-17 cups |
| Saf-instant® yeast | 1 T. | 1½ T. | 2 T. | 4 T. |

\* Use less honey when adding savory ingredients or for bread that's not
as sweet.

1. Mill fresh flour

2. Measure ingredients into bowl, liquids first, then dry ingredients, using only half the flour and adding yeast last

3. Mix gently until the flour is moistened. Continue mixing, adding flour, until the dough cleans the sides and bottom of bowl

4. Knead according to machine - do the gluten window test

5. Divide dough into portions & Deflate

6. Shape into loaves or rolls and place in greased pan(s)

7. Let rise until doubled or 1" above pan

8. Bake at 350° ~30 minutes, until 190° internal temp

9. Cool on cooling racks

10. Slice after 15 minutes, store or freeze after 3-5 hours

No More Bricks!

# Whole Wheat Rye Bread
## Master Recipe

| Yield: Loaves | 1 | 2 | 3 | 6 |
|---|---|---|---|---|
| hot water | 1 cup | 2 cup | 3 cup | 6 cup |
| vegetable oil | 2 T. | ¼ cup | ⅓ cup | ⅔ cup |
| molasses | 2½ T. | ⅓ cup | ½ cup | 1 cup |
| vital wheat gluten | 1 T. | 2 T. | 3 T. | ⅓ cup |
| Dough Enhancer® | 1 tsp. | 2 tsp. | 1 T. | 2 T. |
| sea salt | 1 tsp. | 1½ tsp. | 1 T. | 2 T. |
| freshly-milled rye flour | 1 cup | 2 cups | 3 cups | 6 cups |
| caraway seed (optional) | ½ - 1 T. | 1-2 T. | 2-3 T. | 3-6 T. |
| freshly-milled hard wheat flour | 2-3 cups | 4-5 cups | 6-7 cups | 12-14 cups |
| Saf-Instant® Yeast | 1 T. | 1½ T. | 2 T. | 4 T. |

1. Mill fresh flour

2. Measure ingredients into bowl, liquids first, then dry ingredients, using only half the flour and adding yeast last

3. Mix gently until the flour is moistened. Continue mixing, adding flour, until the dough cleans the sides and bottom of bowl

4. Knead according to machine - do the gluten window test

5. Divide dough into portions & Deflate

6. Shape into loaves or rolls and place in greased pan(s)

7. Let rise until doubled or 1" above pan

8. Bake at 350° ~30 minutes, until 190° internal temp

9. Cool on cooling racks

10. Slice after 15 minutes, store or freeze after 3-5 hours

| Yield: Loaves | 1 | 2 | 3 | 6 |
|---|---|---|---|---|
| Hot Water | ½ cup | 1 cup | 1½ cups | 3 cups |
| Milk | ⅓ cup | ⅔ cup | 1 cup | 2 cups |
| Butter, Soft | 2 T. | ¼ cup | ⅓ cup | ⅔ cup |
| Eggs | 1 | 2 | 3 | 6 |
| Organic Cane Sugar (ECJ) or sugar* | 3 T. | ⅓ cup | ½ cup | 1 cup |
| Vital Wheat Gluten | 1 T. | 2 T. | 3 T. | ⅓ cup |
| Dough Enhancer® | 1 tsp. | 2 tsp. | 1 T. | 2 T. |
| Sea Salt | 1 tsp. | 1½ tsp. | 1 T. | 2 T. |
| Fresh Soft Wheat Flour | 1½ cups | 3 cups | 4½ cups | 9 cups |
| Fresh Hard Wheat Flour** | 1½ - 2 cups | 3 - 4 cups | 4 - 5 cups | 9 - 11 cups |
| Saf-Instant® Yeast | 1 T. | 1½ T. | 2 T. | 4 T. |

*ECJ = Evaporated Cane Juice Crystals, a less-refined sugar.

1. Mill fresh flour

2. Measure ingredients into bowl, liquids first, then dry ingredients, using only half the flour and adding yeast last

3. Mix gently until the flour is moistened. Continue mixing, adding flour, until the dough cleans the sides and bottom of bowl

4. Knead according to machine - do the gluten window test

5. Divide dough into portions & Deflate

6. Shape into loaves or rolls and place in greased pan(s)

7. Let rise until doubled or 1" above pan

8. Bake at 350° ~30 minutes, until 190° internal temp

9. Cool on cooling racks

10. Slice after 15 minutes, store or freeze after 3-5 hours

Recipe _____

Date _____

| Yield: Loaves | 1 | 2 | 3 | 6 |
|---|---|---|---|---|
| | | | | |
| | | | | |
| | | | | |
| | | | | |
| | | | | |
| | | | | |
| | | | | |
| | | | | |
| | | | | |
| | | | | |
| | | | | |

Notes on ingredients, rising time, shaping, taste:

_____

_____

_____

_____

_____

_____

_____

_____

_____

_____

Mix-ins, Knead-ins and Roll-ups

No More Bricks!

## Methods for Forming Loaves

Most of these breads can be adapted to form round loaves, rolls, or buns. There are many more possibilities than I have listed here, so use your imagination or other recipes you have seen to come up with new ingredient combinations and shaping variations. Remember to record your creations on a blank recipe chart for future reference.

There are three possible methods for incorporating additional ingredients into bread dough. I call them "mix-in," "knead-in," and "roll-up." I've assigned each method an icon, so you can see at a glance which one to use with the recipe variations that follow. If there is more than one icon for a given recipe, then choose the one you prefer.

### 1. Mix-in Method

This method calls for adding the extra ingredients during the initial mixing of the bread dough. Just about anything can be added during mixing, but it is especially best to add very wet or moist ingredients, as well as herbs or other seasonings at this time. Additions with sharp edges such as nuts are best added after kneading (see following methods below), to reduce damage to the gluten strands.

With only a few exceptions, I have limited the variations in this book mostly to the knead-in and roll-up methods, in an effort to simplify the number of recipes and to avoid overwhelming the beginning bread baker. But do not let this keep you from experimenting if you wish to do so!

### 2. Knead-in Method

This method can be done either by hand or in the machine. There will be an even dispersal of ingredients throughout the loaf, and they will be visible without having to slice the bread. Some protruding ingredients, such as cheese, may darken significantly during baking; a piece of aluminum foil tented over the loaf may help to reduce this.

Ingredients that will be kneaded in should be relatively dry and no larger than approximately ½" in size. Too many large or wet additions will weigh down the dough and interfere with the rising process. Very moist or wet ingredients are best added using the mix-in method, where their moisture can be balanced out by additional flour.

To knead in by hand, flatten the dough into a disc or rectangle and evenly spread the desired addition(s) on top. Fold the dough over the ingredient(s), and gently begin kneading the dough, folding and refolding, until all additions are incorporated throughout.

To knead in by machine, place the dough and additions back into the mixer, and mix them together until combined. Be careful not to over-knead. Shape the dough into a traditional loaf, round loaf, or other desired shape.

## 3. Roll-up Method

This method takes a little longer to do and re-quires a rolling pin or pastry roller. It will create a spiral effect inside the bread, which is attractive when sliced, and is especially nice for serving guests. It also keeps some of the messier ingredients from browning too much or sticking to the pan. The longer you roll out the dough, the more swirls it will have, but this may also cause it to take longer to rise.

Roll the bread out to a 16" long strip that's about 8" wide. (The width of the strip should be the same as the length of the pan, so it will fit inside when rolled up.) Sprinkle the filling ingredient(s) down the center of the dough and spread them evenly with your fingers. Leave about a one inch margin on all sides; the fill-ing will spread out to the edges as the dough is rolled up. Starting at one 8" edge, roll up the dough to form a loaf, enclosing the ingredients. Pinch both loaf ends to seal the ingredients inside, then pinch the lengthwise seam closed.

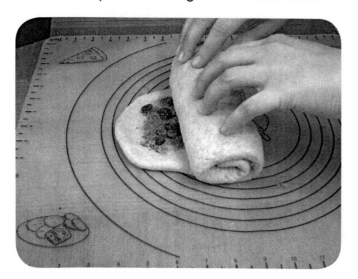

One problem with this method is the "gaps" that sometimes form between the swirls of filling and the baked bread, creating large holes. I have read that this is caused by allowing the bread to rise too long, but it seems to hap-pen to me no matter how careful I am. Most of the time, I just accept the holes, because it's easier. However, if you want to spread butter or a condiment on your bread without it falling through the holes and making a mess, then the only way I know to prevent the problem is to braid the loaf. To do this, prepare your dough with the roll-up method above, except roll the dough from the 16" side, instead of the 8" side. Lengthen this tube into a rope by quickly rock-ing it back and forth, starting at the center and gradually moving your hands outward to the ends while pressing down. When the rope reaches a length of about three to four times the length of your bread pan, cut the dough into three equal pieces and seal each cut end. Braid the pieces together and fold the ends under the loaf. Allow to rise and bake as usual. The bonus for your extra labor is that, besides being gap-free, it makes a very pretty loaf!

### A few tips to keep in mind:

When adding dried fruits, such as raisins, consider soaking them in water or fruit juice until they are plump. This adds flavor, but more importantly, will keep them from absorbing moisture from the bread itself. This way the bread will not dry out as quickly. Make sure to drain them well and pat dry so they don't make the dough soggy.

Choose hard cheeses with a higher melting point such as Cheddar, Swiss, and Parmesan. These can be cubed or shredded, then kneaded into a loaf without melting and running out as goo all over the place. Softer cheeses such as Provolone, Muenster, Monterey Jack, and Mozzarella will work best when rolled up inside the loaf, being contained as a filling.

## Cinnamon Swirl or Cinnamon Raisin Swirl Bread

The flavor of cinnamon rolls with much less time and effort!

   1½ pounds bread dough

   ⅓ cup brown sugar + 1 T cinnamon mixed

   ½ cup raisins (optional)

   ¼ cup chopped nuts (optional)

   powdered sugar glaze (optional)

Use the roll-up method to create the "swirls." Spread the 8x16" strip with cinnamon-sugar mixture (about ¼ to ⅓ cup, or to your taste). If desired, top with raisins and/or chopped nuts. Roll up dough, allow to rise, and bake as usual. When the loaf has cooled for about 20 minutes, drizzle with powdered sugar glaze, if desired.

## Apple Cinnamon Swirl Bread

   1½ pounds bread dough

   ½ cup chopped fresh or dried apples

   cinnamon-sugar mixture

   ½ cup raisins (optional)

   ¼ cup chopped nuts (optional)

Prepare as for Cinnamon Swirl bread, but add apples on top of the cinnamon-sugar mixture, or see note below. Add raisins and/or nuts, if desired.

Note: The moisture from fresh apples will weigh down the bread quite a bit during baking, whereas dried apples will actually absorb some moisture. For best results with fresh apples, add them to the dough during mixing. For a little extra flavor, substitute apple juice for part of the liquid and decrease sugar accordingly.

## Mock Rye Bread

The flavor of rye in a 100% wheat bread

   1½ pounds bread dough

   ½ to 1 tablespoon caraway seeds

   1 teaspoon anise seeds (optional)

Use the mix-in or knead-in method to add the caraway and anise seeds into the dough. After rising, glaze with egg wash and sprinkle with additional seeds, if desired.

## Marble Rye Bread

This bread is pictured on the front cover

- ¾ pound (12 oz.) wheat, Kamut®, or spelt dough

- ¾ pound (12 oz.) rye dough (with or without caraway seeds)

Roll out each portion of dough into an 8 x 16" strip. Place one strip of dough on top of the other, and roll them up together to form one loaf, pinching the edges to seal.

If making more than one loaf, alternate using the darker dough on the outside of one, and the lighter dough on the outside of the other for two different looks.

## Crunchy Birdseed Bread

This is my son Weston's favorite bread, and it makes excellent toast

- 1½ pounds bread dough

- ½ cup seeds and/or cracked grains of choice

Use the knead-in method to add the seeds and/or grains. Use whatever you like or happen to have on hand, layering several different kinds into a ½ cup measuring cup until it's full. Choices include: cracked 9-grain mix or any cracked grain, bulgur, millet, regular or golden flax seeds, raw sunflower seeds, raw pumpkin seeds, amaranth, etc. The more colors and sizes of seeds there are, the more attractive the bread will be. This bread will not rise quite as high and light, because the grains and seeds will damage the gluten strands. It may also have "torn" spots on the surface.

Note: At nearly every class where I demonstrate this bread, I am asked if actual bird seed is used for this recipe! No, this is just what my kids call it because of how it looks. Always pur-

chase grains and seeds that are intended for human consumption only.

## Cheesy Onion Bread

- 1½ pounds bread dough

- 1 cup shredded cheese, sharp cheddar or your favorite

- ⅓ cup to ½ cup finely chopped onion

Use either the knead in or roll-up method to incorporate the cheese and onions. In the last few minutes of baking, garnish with additional shredded cheese, if desired.

## Olive Bread or Cheesy Olive Bread

This bread is pictured on the front cover

- 1½ pounds bread dough

- ½-1 cup green or black olives, or combination

- ½ cup shredded cheese, optional

- ¼ cup diced onions, optional

Olives may be whole, sliced, or chopped, but make sure they are very well drained and patted dry. For added flavor, extra-virgin olive oil can be substituted for the oil in the initial mixing of the dough. Using the knead-in method with whole olives gives more of a European flair, especially when shaped into a round loaf (boule) or batard (torpedo-shaped loaf). The roll-up method is especially attractive and is even more interesting with chopped olives, mixed with shredded cheese and diced onions. After rising, glaze with egg wash and garnish with additional sliced olives, if desired.

## Cranberry Pecan Bread or Cranberry Walnut Bread

Delicious for a turkey sandwich

  1½ pounds bread dough

  ½ cup sweetened dried cranberries

  ¼ to ⅓ cup chopped pecans or walnuts

Use either the knead-in or roll-up method to add cranberries and nuts to the dough.

## Jalapeño Jack Bread

  1½ pounds bread dough

  ⅓ cup shredded Monterrey Jack or Pepper Jack cheese

  2 tablespoons to - ¼ cup finely chopped jalapeño slices (or to taste)

  corn meal, optional

Use the roll-up method for adding cheese and peppers. Wear gloves or use extreme caution when handling hot peppers. If desired, roll the loaf in freshly milled corn meal before placing in a greased pan.

## Three Cheese Bread

  1½ pounds bread dough

  ¼ cup Romano cheese

  ¼ cup Parmesan cheese

  ¼ cup Asiago cheese

Use either the knead-in or roll-up method to add the cheese to the dough. Cut the cheese into ½" cubes to be kneaded in, or grate the cheese to make a roll-up loaf.

## Italian Bread

  1 tablespoon dried basil

  1 tablespoon oregano

  2 garlic cloves, crushed

  ½ cup grated Parmesan cheese

Use the mix-in method to add the above ingredients to each loaf (or to every 3 cups of flour in your recipe). Use the lesser amount of sugar and substitute olive oil for vegetable oil if desired. Makes great bread sticks!

## Spelt Bread

This can also be used as a master recipe.

Use any of the master recipes, but substitute spelt flour for the wheat flour. It will take a little bit more spelt flour to equal the same amount of wheat flour, but you have learned to make bread without measuring the flour, letting the dough tell you when enough has been added.

If you're trying to reduce your intake of gluten, you can omit the vital wheat gluten in the master recipe. The bread will not rise as high and will have a denser texture. Note that spelt itself is not gluten-free.

## Kamut® Bread

This can also be used as a master recipe.

Use any of the master recipes, but substitute Kamut® flour for the wheat flour.

Kamut® flour is my favorite – it makes a beautiful golden loaf, with a very soft texture, almost cake-like.

If you're trying to reduce your intake of gluten, you can omit the vital wheat gluten in the master recipe. The bread will not rise as high and will have a denser texture. Note that Kamut® itself is not gluten-free.

No More Bricks!

Creative Dinner Rolls

Hamburger Buns & More

Bread Bowls

No More Bricks!

## Creative Dinner Rolls

My family loves to eat rolls - something about those little individual "packages" seems to make them taste better! They're great to grab for a quick breakfast or lunch on the run, along with some fruit and cheese.

If you weigh each piece of dough so that they're equal, they'll all bake at the same rate. Then, form a round roll by stretching each piece of dough outward from the center, and tucking the edges underneath to be pinched and sealed. This takes a bit more time, but results in more even rising, and a rounder shape. Since bread tends to rise more in the center, in most cases you'll want to then flatten the roll or bun slightly with your fingers to create a gentle dome, instead of a big round ball. In the case of bread bowls, the height in the center is what you want, so don't flatten those.

Remember that the type of pan you use affects the crust. For soft rolls, use a bright shiny metal pan. I like to use parchment paper for all my rolls, as the lack of oil spray keeps them softer and the paper slides quickly off the baking sheet and onto a cooling rack. The parchment can be reused a few times for successive batches.

For browner or crisper rolls, use a well-greased dark, non-stick pan or stoneware pan. Place the rolls 3" apart. The more oil on the pan, the crisper the bottoms will be.

For rolls that pull apart (similar to packaged rolls and buns) place each one a finger's width apart. During rising and baking they will fill in the spaces and touch each other. Otherwise, place rolls 3" apart so that they will brown evenly on all sides.

Allow rolls to rise until they appear to have nearly doubled in size. Glaze with egg wash for a shiny, golden finish. Sprinkle with seeds or other garnish, if desired.

Bake at 350° for 15-25 minutes, depending on size. Rolls should be golden brown; test the internal temperature to verify they are completely done. After baking, remove rolls from the pan at once and serve immediately or allow to cool on a rack. Buns and bowls should be cooled before slicing open.

Because of their small size, rolls and buns can dry out more quickly. To freshen leftovers, wrap each roll individually in a paper towel and microwave it for a few seconds. The towel keeps it from drying out and becoming hard.

There are endless possibilities for shapes of rolls. Most of these start with either a round ball or a rope. Since it takes longer to do, I always enlist the help of my kids, who love to make all kinds of creative shapes.

## Clover Leaf Rolls

Divide 1½ pounds of dough into 24-36 pieces. Shape each piece into a ball, and place three balls together in each section of a greased muffin pan.

Depending on the size of your muffin cups, you may need to alter the size of your dough balls to make sure they rise up nice and tall .

## Knots, Coils, and Braids

Divide 1½ pounds of dough into portions of 2-3 ounces each, depending on desired roll size. Roll each one into a 9" to 12" rope. Here are just a few ideas for shapes with ropes:

- Tie the rope into a loose knot

- Tie a knot and tuck one end over the top and through the middle hole, then tuck the other end underneath forming a rosette

- Coil it around itself in a spiral circle

- Coil each end toward the center, like the letter C

- Coil each end toward the center, in opposite directions, like letter S

- Make an open circle, like a bagel, pinching the ends together

- Twist an open circle in half, creating a figure 8

- Fold the rope in half, onto itself, and twist it

- Make three ropes of equal size and braid them together

- Twist the rope and lay it out straight for a breadstick

## Crescent Rolls

Roll 1½ pounds of dough into a 15" circle. Brush with softened or melted butter, if desired. Use a knife or pizza cutter to cut the circle into 12 triangular wedges, pizza-style. Starting with the wide edge, roll each triangle toward the point at the center. Place each roll onto a greased or parchment-lined baking sheet, and curve them slightly to resemble a crescent.

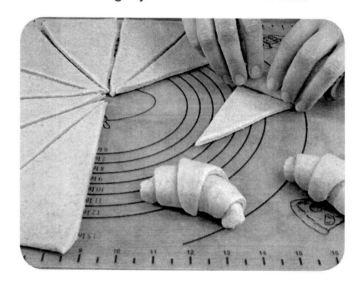

No More Bricks!

## Hamburger, Hot Dog, & Sub Sandwich Buns

Divide 1½ pounds of dough into 8 equal pieces for a 3-ounce bun, or 6 equal pieces for a larger 4-ounce bun. For traditional hamburger buns, use the stretch-tuck-and-pinch method for creating a round roll. Place on a greased or parchment paper-lined baking sheet and flatten with your fingers (otherwise it will be tall like a bread bowl). Cover and allow to rise until doubled; glaze with egg wash and sprinkle with sesame seeds or poppy seeds, if desired. Bake at 350° for ~20 minutes.

For a Kaiser-style bun, use a 4-ounce piece of dough and shape it into a 12" rope. Tie the rope into a knot; tuck one loose end over the top and through the middle hole, then tuck the other end underneath. Proceed as for traditional hamburger buns.

For hot dog buns, roll each piece of dough into a cylinder approximately 2" wide by 5" long. Place each on a greased or parchment paper-lined baking sheet and flatten. Allow to rise and bake as for hamburger buns.

For sub sandwich buns, prepare as for hot dog buns, except divide each loaf portion into 2-4 pieces (or use the entire loaf), depending on size of sandwich desired. Use the stretch-tuck-and-pinch method to shape into a cylinder for more even rising and baking. Allow to rise until doubled; glaze and garnish if desired. Bake at 350° for 20-30 minutes, depending on size.

## Party Dip Bowls or Large Soup Bowls

Shape 1½ pounds of bread dough into one round loaf, as above. Place on greased or parchment-paper lined baking sheet. Allow to rise until doubled; glaze and garnish if desired. Bake at 350° for 30-35 minutes, or until internal temperature reaches 190°. After cooling, slice a lid off the top, jack-o-lantern style. Holding a serrated knife vertically, cut around the edges of inside of the loaf, but not all the way through the bottom. Carefully pull out the center portion of bread and cut it into 1" cubes for dipping (these can also be toasted for croutons). Fill with creamy soup, stew, chili, pasta, salad, or party dip.

## Individual Soup, Salad, or Pasta Bowls

Same as above, but divide 1½ pounds of dough into 4 equal pieces. Form into four rounds and place each on a greased or parchment paper-lined baking sheet at least 3" apart. Allow to rise until doubled; glaze with egg wash if desired. Bake at 350° for 20 minutes, or until internal temperature reaches 190°.

3 Ways to Bake a Pizza

Veggie & Fruit Pizzas

Calzones

Stromboli 4 Ways

Bread Crust Pot Pies

Pigs-in-a-Blanket

Pocket Sandwiches

No More Bricks!

One of the perks of preparing bread dough in bulk is that there are a number of convenient meals that can be made from it. While several of these are essentially the same thing – a baked sandwich – forming them in different shapes, using interchangeable ingredients, and calling them different names can make them seem like a completely new meal. At least that's what I've led my family to believe, so don't tell my secret! And I must admit, it makes things a little more interesting for me as well.

## Pizza

The making of pizza is truly an artform unto itself, and I don't pretend to do any kind of justice to it in this short section. In truth, bread dough is not the optimal thing to use for pizza, but it is handy, especially when you're already making bread anyway. This version of whole grain pizza will be a little more bready, less crunchy-chewy than traditional white-flour pizza, but is a decent time- and money-saving substitute. These techniques help make it crisp on the bottom, eliminating the limp, soggy crusts of some recipes I've tried in the past.

### To Prepare The Dough For Baking

The amount of dough you use for each pizza (1 to 1½ pounds) varies according to the size of your pan or stone, and how thick you like the crust. For example, I like to use one pound of dough for a 12" pizza with a medium-thin crust, about ¼" to ⅜" thick. If your pan is larger or you like your crust thicker, then use 1½ pounds of dough.

Roll or gently stretch dough to desired size and thickness. Prick crust all over with a fork (called "docking") and let rise, covered, for 15-30 minutes. Optional – brush the risen dough with a thin coating of olive oil, to further protect the crust from soaking up too much sauce and becoming soggy. Choose your baking method from the options below.

### 3 Ways to Bake a Pizza

### Option 1 – Fully cook

Top the unbaked dough with sauce and toppings all at once; bake until golden brown and bubbly.

### Option 2 – Par-bake crust to use now or freeze for later

After the dough has risen, bake it just until the crust is set. Add sauce, toppings, and cheese; return to oven and bake until golden brown and bubbly. This works well if you like to add a lot of sauce and toppings, because it helps prevent the crust from being too soggy and gummy. Or, to freezer for later use, remove par-baked crust from oven to a wire rack; cool completely. Wrap well and freeze (see Tips chapter). To serve, thaw crust, add sauce, toppings, and cheese, and complete final baking.

### Option 3 – Pre-baked crust for cold fruit or veggie pizza

Fully bake the crust so that cold or room-temperature toppings can be added later. Lift the edge of the crust with a long-handled utensil; it should be browned to the center. Remove from stone or pan to cooling rack.

### Baking Stone vs. Pizza Pan

Using a preheated stone puts the dough in immediate, direct contact with high heat; this "sears" the crust, making it crispy on the bottom while soft on the inside. Place your stone in a cold oven and preheat it at 400° to 450° for at least 30 minutes, but preferably an hour. Slide the pizza directly onto the stone and bake until brown and bubbly.

If you prefer to use a pizza pan, liberally grease it with oil or a combination of oil and lecithin. The more oil you use, the more the bottom crust will "fry" for crispiness and flavor (and oops, calories!). When the dough is ready to bake, set the pan on the oven rack or directly on top of a preheated stone.

### Transferring the Dough

Forget what you've heard about using cornmeal or flour to effortlessly transfer dough from here to there at will! After cleaning up the remains of many misshapen pizzas splattered all over my oven and kitchen floor, not to mention piles of smelly, burned cornmeal, I can tell you this is NOT a reliable method – it's just a big mess. Instead, roll the dough out on a piece of parchment paper, then slide a pizza peel underneath and transfer it, paper and all, onto the stone. If your oven is heated to 400° or less, you can fully bake the crust on the parchment paper. At higher temperatures, you may want to carefully

reach into the oven with a pair of tongs and pull the parchment out from under the pizza, as soon as the crust has set, because the edges of the paper may begin to char and smoke.

To transfer dough to a pizza pan, pick up the dough by the parchment paper, flip it over upside down into the well-greased pan, then peel the paper off. Don't bake the paper in the pan.

### Baking Time and Temperature

The baking time depends on your choice of pan, oven temperature, and how thick your pizza is – both crust and toppings. Watch your crust carefully and check it periodically for doneness. Use a long-handled utensil to carefully lift the bottom of the pizza and peek underneath. It should be browned completely to the center. The top should be bubbly and the cheese golden brown. If par-baking, the crust should be set (firm enough to hold its shape when moved), but not too brown yet. It will brown more with subsequent baking.

## Traditional Pizza

1 – 1½ pounds bread dough

½ cup pizza sauce, more or less to taste

toppings of choice, see below

No More Bricks!

½ – 1 cup shredded cheese

Pizza toppings:

crumbled cooked ground beef or sausage

shredded cooked BBQ beef or chicken

pepperoni or ham slices

pineapple tidbits

red or green onions

mushrooms

bell peppers

cherry tomatoes

green or black olives

artichoke hearts, drained

chopped spinach leaves

olive oil and basil leaves

Preheat the oven to 400° or 450°. Roll dough on a parchment-paper lined pizza peel, or inside a pizza pan. Dock the crust, cover it, and let it rise for 15-30 minutes. Spread the crust with sauce and add toppings. Sprinkle with cheese and bake until golden brown.

# Breakfast Pizza

1½ pounds bread dough

6 eggs

½ cup milk

½ teaspoon dry mustard

¼ cup minced green onions

salt & pepper to taste

½ - 1 cup bacon or sausage, cooked & crumbled

2 cups frozen hash browns

½ - ¾ cup shredded cheddar or Monterey Jack cheese

Preheat oven to 400°. Roll out dough inside a well-greased deep dish pizza pan or 10x15 jelly roll pan. Dock, cover, and let rise for 15-30 minutes. Par-bake dough for 5-7 minutes, or until the crust is set. Meanwhile, beat eggs with milk, dry mustard, onions, salt, and pepper in a medium bowl. Layer cooked meat and potatoes over par-baked crust. Pour egg mixture over all and season with salt & pepper to taste. Bake for 20 minutes, or until eggs are almost set. Add shredded cheese and continue baking 5-10 minutes more, or until eggs are cooked and cheese is melted.

# Cool Veggie Patch Pizza

Pre-baked pizza crust, cooled

½ cup Ranch salad dressing or cream cheese flavored with onion, garlic, or herbs

2-3 cups sliced, shredded, or bite-sized raw vegetables of choice: red or green onions, broccoli, cauliflower, bell peppers, olives, mushrooms, carrots, zucchini, sprouts, avocados, cherry tomatoes, spinach leaves, fresh herbs

1 cup grated cheese(s) of choice

Spread salad dressing or cream cheese on pizza crust. Top with veggies and follow with a sprinkling of your favorite grated cheeses, such as mozzarella, provolone, and Parmesan. Serve immediately.

# Cold Fruit Pizza

Pre-baked pizza crust, cooled

12-16 ounces soft flavored cream cheese (strawberry, honey, etc.)

2 cups fresh sliced fruit: bananas, apples, peaches, pineapples, berries, etc.

½ cup toasted nuts, optional

¼ cup shredded coconut, optional

Spread cream cheese over cooled pizza crust. Top with fruit and sprinkle with nuts or coconut, if desired.


# Calzones

Traditionally a pizza turnover, these can be made with any filling inside.

1½ pounds bread dough

choice of filling (see below)

choice of sliced or shredded cheese

pizza sauce, salsa, or dressing for dipping

You can spread sauce inside the calzone underneath the filling, but I prefer to serve it on the side for dipping to prevent sogginess, especially for leftovers or freezing.

### To form one large calzone:

Pat or roll the dough into a 15" circle. If using pizza sauce, spread it evenly over one half of the circle, leaving a 1" border around the edge. Add filling over sauce, if using, and top with cheese. Gently lift and stretch the other half of the circle over the filling, laying it just ½" short of the other edge. Fold the extra dough over the seam and press the edges of the dough together with a fork to seal. Use a knife to cut slits in the top to allow steam to escape. Cover and allow to rise for 15-20 minutes. If desired, glaze with egg wash; garnish with seeds and herbs, or sprinkle with coarse salt.

### To form individual calzones:

Divide dough into six 4-ounce portions. Roll each piece into a 9" circle, then fill, seal, and slit as above. Cover and allow to rise 15-20 minutes; glaze.

### To bake:

Bake calzones on a parchment-lined baking sheet or baking stone at 400° for 15-25 minutes, depending on size. Serve with sauce or dressing for dipping.

### Filling ideas:

pizza toppings

cooked chili, taco, or Sloppy Joe meat

meatballs, olives , and parmesan

leftover sliced roast beef, chicken, or turkey

assorted sliced deli meats

smoked sausage and bell peppers

ricotta cheese and chopped spinach

Philly cheesesteak – sliced beef, carmelized onions, mushrooms, peppers

Reuben fixings – corned beef, sauerkraut, Swiss cheese (use rye or mock rye dough, or sprinkle with caraway seeds)

**Stromboli :** a baked sandwich with fun shaping options...

  1½ pounds bread dough

  Choice of filling options (see above)

  Sauce, salsa, or dressing for dipping

Roll dough into a 12x16" rectangle. Place filling ingredients evenly over the dough, leaving a clean 1" border on one long edge. Roll the dough up into a cylinder, toward the clean edge, and pinch to seal. If there's a larger "hump" in the middle, gently squeeze it out to the sides. Place one hand at each end of the roll and push it toward the center of the roll to even up the sides and ensure equal filling. You can leave the roll in a straight line, form it into a circle, or see other creative shaping options below. Cover loosely with greased plastic wrap and let rise about 30 minutes, or until doubled. Glaze with egg wash; garnish with seeds or herbs. Bake at 350° for 35 minutes, or until golden brown.

**Stromboli Twist:** Prepare Stromboli as above, but after rolling into a cylinder, slice the cylinder in half lengthwise. Lay each half next to each other, cut side facing up. Twist the two halves together, keeping the cut sides up. Pinch each end and tuck under slightly. Cover loosely with greased plastic wrap and let rise about 30 minutes, or until nearly doubled. Glaze with egg wash; garnish with seeds or herbs. Bake at 350° for 25-30 minutes, or until golden brown.

**Stromboli Spirals:** Prepare Stromboli as above, but cut cylinder into 2" slices with a serrated knife. Lay each roll on a parchment-lined baking sheet and flatten slightly with your fingers. Cover loosely with greased plastic wrap and let rise about 30 minutes, or until doubled. Bake at 350° for 20-25 minutes until golden brown. I often freeze baked spirals for later use - see the special freezing directions under Freezer Sandwiches in the Tips chapter.

**Lattice Stromboli:** Roll out dough as for traditional Stromboli, but place filling ingredients across the middle third of the dough only. Along each side of the filling, cut perpendicular strips 1½" apart, almost up to the edge of the filling. Beginning at one end, crisscross strips of dough over the filling, and pinch to seal at each end. Cover loosely with greased plastic wrap and let rise about 30 minutes, or until doubled. Glaze with egg wash; garnish with seeds or herbs. Bake at 350° for 25-30 minutes until golden brown.

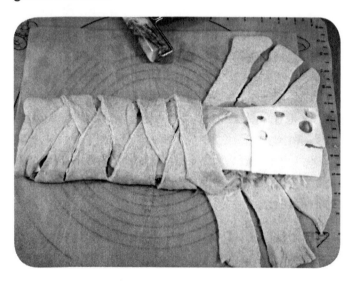

# Bread Crust Pot Pie

Using bread dough instead of pie crust cuts down on fat and saves calories. Make the filling in bulk and store it in the freezer.

1½ pounds bread dough*

pot pie filling (recipe follows)

1 egg

1 tablespoon water

*Be sure to use the lesser amount of sugar in the dough for this recipe. Otherwise the sweetness is too pronounced and doesn't blend well with the savory filling.

Divide dough into a ½ pound portion and a 1 pound portion. Roll out the larger piece to cover the bottom and sides of a well-greased 9x9 pan, allowing the dough to overhang the sides, as for pie crust. Spoon in pot pie filling. Roll the remaining dough into a rectangle and lay over the filling to form the top crust. Fold the bottom crust over the top crust; pinch or press together with a fork to seal. Brush the dough with egg wash, and cut several slits to allow steam to escape. Bake at 375° for 30-40 minutes until golden brown.

## Chicken, Turkey, or Beef Pot Pie Filling

⅓ cup butter

1¾ cups chicken, turkey, or beef broth

⅓ cup flour

⅔ cup milk

⅓ cup chopped onion

2 cups cooked cubed chicken, turkey, roast

½ teaspoon salt

beef, or browned ground beef

¼ teaspoon pepper

10 ounce package frozen vegetables

Make a white sauce by melting butter in a saucepan. Add flour, onion, salt & pepper, and stir constantly until smooth and bubbly. Stir in broth and milk; bring to a boil and cook one minute. Stir in meat and vegetables (see note) until heated through.

Note: To freeze the filling, prepare as above, but do not add the frozen vegetables until the meat mixture has been chilled and is ready to go in the freezer. This prevents the veggies from thawing and refreezing. Place the mixture in a freezer bag. Flatten the filled bag into a thin layer for quick freezing and thawing.

## Pigs-in-a-Blanket

1½ pounds bread dough

12-18 hot dogs or sausages, depending on size

fresh cornmeal for rolling, optional

popsicle sticks, optional

Roll the dough into a 12 x 16" rectangle. With a pizza wheel, cut dough into strips that will fit around your meat, approximately 2"x5" for regular-length hot dogs, or 2"x6" for bun-length dogs. Alternatively, let the kids make ropes out of dough and twirl them around the hot dogs.

Wrap each strip or rope of dough around a piggy, and roll it in cornmeal, if desired. Place the piggies on a greased cookie sheet; cover with a towel and allow to rise for 20-30 minutes. Bake at 350° for 15-20 minutes, or until golden brown. After baking, insert a popsicle stick into each Piggy for easy handling.

To freeze baked piggies, wrap individually in foil and place in a freezer storage bag. To serve, thaw in the foil. Reheat on a parchment-paper lined baking sheet at 350° until heated through.

## Pocket Sandwiches

These could be made in a skillet, but a sandwich maker cuts and seals the edges of the sandwich to contain the filling in little pockets

thinly sliced bread

softened butter

choice of filling

**savory fillings:**

leftover chili, taco, or sloppy Joe meat

deli meat and cheese

tuna or chicken salad

cheese and sliced tomatoes

cooked scrambled eggs & crumbled bacon

**sweet fillings: (my kids call these home-made PopTarts)**

cinnamon & sugar + pat of butter

cocoa & sugar + pat of butter

thinly sliced apples + cinnamon

jam or jelly

pudding or pie filling

Use an electric knife to slice the bread thinly and evenly. Butter two slices of bread for each sandwich (my machine makes 2 sandwiches at once). Place one piece buttered side down on the grill, and add filling(s). Top with the other piece of bread, buttered side up. Close the machine and grill according to manufacturer's instructions. These could be made in bulk and frozen, but would need to be reheated in the oven or toaster oven to crisp up again.

I went shopping to replace my waffle iron, and found a combination sandwich griller & waffle maker. It includes a set of 4 interchangeable grill plates that pop out and go in the dishwasher for easy cleanup. My kids love to invent their own concoctions for breakfast, lunch, or dessert, and I love that they are making it themselves – less work for me! For many more creative sandwich filling ideas, check out a cute little cookbook called New Recipes from Your Sandwich Maker, by Donna Rathmell German (Bristol Publishing, 2003).

Sweet Rolls 3 Ways

Tea Rings

Doughnuts

Sticky Picky 5 Ways

Fruit Kuchen

Better Butter Spreads

 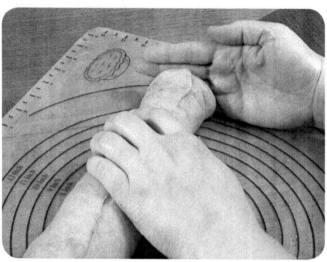

No More Bricks!

## Classic Cinnamon Rolls

1½ pounds bread dough

½ cup cinnamon-sugar mixture (see below)

½ cup raisins, optional

½ cup chopped nuts, optional

frosting or glaze, optional

Roll the dough into a 12" x 16" rectangle on a sheet of parchment paper. Leaving a 1" border on one long side, brush with melted butter or margarine and sprinkle with ½ cup (or to taste) cinnamon-sugar mixture. Add a layer of raisins and/or nuts, if desired. Roll up the dough starting opposite of the unbuttered edge, using the parchment paper to help lift the dough as you roll. Pull the free edge up over the roll, and pinch together to seal.

Manipulate the roll so that it is of a uniform diameter. This will make rolls that are all the same size, with equal filling. If there is a larger "hump" in the middle, gently squeeze it out to the sides. Place one hand at each end of the roll and push it toward the center of the roll to even up the sides. Don't be afraid to pick up each end and push it toward the center if it is too long and thin. This should result in a cylinder of fairly equal size all the way across.

Slice with a serrated knife into 2" slices, which should yield 8 rolls. Place each roll onto a parchment-paper lined or greased baking sheet, and press the rolls down with your fingers to flatten slightly. Cover, let rise until doubled, and bake at 350° for 20-25 minutes, or until golden brown. Spread the tops with butter if desired. After 20 minutes of cooling, spread baked rolls with icing or glaze.

### Cinnamon-Sugar Mixture

1 cup brown sugar or sucanat

¼ cup ground cinnamon

Stir sugar and cinnamon together, storing any unused portion in an airtight container on the shelf. This is a more potent blend of cinnamon than usual, because more spice is required for whole wheat dough than white bread dough, as it tends to mask the flavors. I like to make a triple batch to keep on hand for cinnamon rolls, cinnamon toast, French toast, etc.

### Cream Cheese Icing

8 ounces cream cheese, softened

1 tablespoon milk

1 teaspoon Vanilla

4 cups powdered sugar

Beat cream cheese, milk, and vanilla together until smooth. Gradually beat in powdered sugar, one cup at a time until desired consistency is reached.

### Vanilla Glaze

⅓ cup melted butter

2 cups powdered sugar

1½ teaspoon vanilla

2-4 tablespoons hot water or milk

Mix butter, sugar, and vanilla together. Stir in water or milk, one teaspoon at a time until desired consistency. Tip: mix glaze together in a large, liquid measuring cup for easy pouring over rolls.

# Rise & Shine Orange Rolls

Prepare as for cinnamon rolls, but substitute orange-sugar mixture for the cinnamon-sugar. These rolls will be gooey, so either bake them in a 9x13" pan, or follow these directions to use a jellyroll pan. To help keep the filling from oozing out, make a "floor" for the bottom of each roll. Instead of fully rolling the dough into a log, stop rolling when there is 2" left to go of the long side of the rectangle. Slice into 2" rolls; each one will have a 2" long "tail." Slightly stretch and wrap the tail under the bottom of each roll, enclosing the filling. Pinch seams to seal, leaving top exposed as usual. Cover, allow to rise, and bake at 350° for 20-25 minutes, or until golden brown. Spread the tops with butter if desired. After 20 minutes of cooling, drizzle baked rolls with Orange Glaze.

## Orange-Sugar Mixture

½ cup brown sugar or sucanat + 1½ tablespoons fresh orange zest

Stir sugar and zest together, storing any unused portion in the refrigerator.

## Citrus Glaze

⅓ cup melted butter

1 teaspoon fresh orange or lemon zest

2 cups powdered sugar

2-4 tablespoons orange or lemon juice

Stir orange zest into hot butter, allowing to steep a few minutes to infuse the orange flavor. Add powdered sugar and mix. Stir in orange juice, 1 teaspoon at a time until desired consistency is reached.

# Cozy Cocoa Rolls

Prepare as for cinnamon rolls, but substitute cocoa-sugar mixture for the cinnamon-sugar. If desired, sprinkle some chocolate chips or chopped baker's chocolate over the sugar mixture. These rolls will be gooey, so either bake them in a 9x13" pan, or follow these directions to use a jellyroll pan. To help keep the chocolate from oozing out the bottom, make a "floor" for the bottom of each roll. Instead of fully rolling the dough into a log, stop rolling when there is 2" left to go of the long side of the rectangle. Slice into 2" rolls; each one will have a 2" long "tail." Slightly stretch and wrap the tail under the bottom of each roll, enclosing the filling. Pinch seams to seal, leaving top exposed as usual. Slightly stretch and wrap the tail under the bottom of each roll, enclosing the filling. Pinch to seal all around. Cover and allow to rise until doubled. Bake at 350° for 20-25 minutes, or until golden brown. Spread the tops with butter if desired. After cooling for at least 20 minutes, drizzle baked rolls with Chocolate or Coffee Glaze.

## Cocoa-Sugar Mixture

½ cup brown sugar or sucanat + ¼ cup unsweetened cocoa powder

¼ cup semisweet chocolate chips, if desired

## Chocolate Glaze

½ cup semisweet chocolate chips

2 tablespoons butter

2 tablespoons corn syrup

Melt chocolate chips, butter, and corn syrup together in a small bowl in the microwave for a few seconds at a time and stir. Continue heating and stirring until the mixture is smooth, being careful not to scorch the chocolate.

### Coffee Glaze

⅓ cup melted butter

2 cups powdered sugar

2-4 T brewed coffee

Mix melted butter, sugar, and vanilla. Stir in coffee, one teaspoon at a time, until desired consistency is reached.

## Tea Rings

## Citrus Tea Ring

A variation on the cinnamon roll, with a creamy filling and an elegant presentation

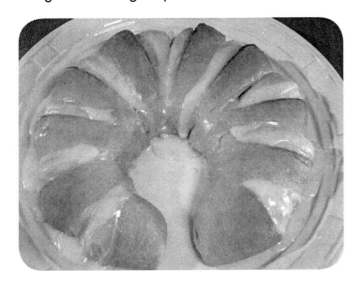

1½ pounds bread dough

Filling:

8 oz. cream cheese, softened

¼ cup ECJ crystals (sugar)

1 egg

2 teaspoon fresh orange or lemon zest

2 tablespoon soft wheat flour

### Citrus Glaze

In a medium bowl, mix the cream cheese and sugar; add remaining ingredients and stir until smooth. Chill until ready to use.

Roll the dough into a 10" x 16" rectangle on a sheet of parchment paper. Spread with filling, leaving a ½" border on one long side. Roll up the dough starting opposite of the clean edge, using the parchment paper to help lift the dough as you roll. Pull the free edge up over the roll, and pinch together to seal.

Place the entire roll onto a greased or parchment-paper lined baking sheet and coil into a circle or horseshoe shape. Cover with greased plastic wrap and place in the refrigerator to chill until the filling is firm, about 15 minutes. Score the ring with a knife every 1½" to 2". With kitchen shears or a serrated knife, carefully slice about ¾ of the way through the roll, leaving each section attached, but exposing the filling. Do not cut the slices all the way through. Repeat cuts on score marks all the way around the ring. Cover and allow to rise until doubled; bake at 350° for about 35 minutes. If the top begins to get too brown, tent it with some aluminum foil. Glaze after 20 minutes of cooling.

## Cinnamon Tea Ring

1½ pounds bread dough

Cinnamon-sugar mixture

Glaze of choice

Prepare as for cinnamon rolls. After rolling up and pinching sealed, form the cylinder into a ring, as for the citrus tea ring, but omit chilling time. Score and make cuts around the ring. Pick up each slice and twist it 90º to lie flat on the pan. Cover and allow to rise until doubled; bake at 350˚ for about 30 minutes. Glaze after 20 minutes of cooling.

## Doughnuts

1½ pounds bread dough

Vegetable oil for deep frying

Powdered sugar, cinnamon sugar, or glaze of choice

Roll out dough to a ½" thickness on an oiled surface. Use a doughnut cutter to cut out doughnuts and doughnut holes and place them on a parchment paper-lined baking sheet. Cover with a towel and allow to rise for about 30 minutes, or until doubled in size. Meanwhile, heat 2-3" of oil in a large saucepan or pot over medium-high heat. Test oil by carefully dropping in one doughnut hole. The oil should bubble up around it as the "hole" floats. Add a few additional doughnuts or holes to fry. Work quickly and turn each one over after it fries briefly, as they overbrown easily. When doughnuts are golden brown on both sides, drain them briefly on layers of paper towels. Drop them into a plastic bag of sugar, shaking to coat. Or, dip them in a bowl of glaze. Place glazed doughnuts on cooling racks with a pan underneath to catch the drips. These are best when served warm, but they may be refreshed by just a few seconds in the microwave.

## Sticky Picky

A.k.a. Monkey Bread or Bubble Bread, make it sweet or savory, according to your mood. Better yet, make one of each!

1½ pounds bread dough

½ cup melted butter (1 stick)

¾ cup sugar mixture (see below)

½ cup chopped nuts, optional

Powdered sugar glaze, optional

Sprinkle ¼ cup of the nuts, if using, in the bottom of a greased Bundt® pan or ring mold. Cut the dough into 48 pieces. Roll each piece into a ball and dip in melted butter, then roll in desired sugar mixture. Place half of the dough balls on top of nuts; layer with remaining nuts and dough balls. Let rise until doubled and bake at 350° for 30 minutes, or until golden brown. If the butter starts to brown too much, cover loosely with aluminum foil in the last 10 minutes of baking. Immediately invert onto a serving plate and drizzle with a powdered sugar glaze, if desired.

## Cinnamon Sticky Picky

Cinnamon-sugar mixture:

¾ cup brown sugar or sucanat

3 T cinnamon

## Chocolate Sticky Picky

1½ cups milk chocolate chips

Cocoa-sugar mixture:

¾ cup brown sugar or sucanat

2 T unsweetened cocoa powder

Roll each dough ball around a few chocolate chips before dipping in butter and rolling in sugar.

## Orange Sticky Picky

Orange-sugar mixture:

¾ cup brown sugar or sucanat

2 T fresh orange zest

⅔ cup orange marmalade

3 T melted butter

Prepare dough balls according to original recipe. In a bowl, stir ⅔ cup orange marmalade with 3 T melted butter. Pour half of this over the first layer of dough, followed by the rest on top of the last layer of dough. Alternatively, skip this step and drizzle baked Sticky Picky with Orange Glaze from the cinnamon roll recipe.

## Garlic & Herb Sticky Picky

½ cup melted butter

2 T fresh minced parsley

1-2 teaspoon minced garlic

2 teaspoons poppy seeds

½ cup chopped green onion

Combine butter, parsley, and garlic in a small bowl. Dip dough balls in herb butter and place in pan. Sprinkle green onion and poppy seeds between layers of dough.

## Pepperoni Sticky Picky

4 oz. pepperoni slices, chopped

4 oz. string cheese, cubed

½ cup olive oil or melted butter

pizza sauce for dipping

Wrap each dough ball around a small amount of pepperoni and cheese, sealing it inside. Dip each ball in butter or olive oil and roll in Parmesan cheese. After baking, serve with pizza sauce for dipping.

## Fruit Kuchen

A mildly sweet breakfast or dessert with a fruit and custard filling.

1 pound soft wheat egg dough (or any master dough)

1 quart fresh, frozen, or canned fruit

3 eggs

1-2 tablespoons + ½ cup sugar, divided

½ cup heavy whipping cream

1½ teaspoon vanilla

Roll the dough inside a well-greased 9x13" casserole dish, covering the bottom and allowing dough to go up the sides of the pan slightly. Cover and let rise 20-30 minutes.

Meanwhile, if the fruit needs sweetening, toss it with 1-2 tablespoon sugar in a small bowl and set aside. In medium-sized bowl, beat the eggs and sugar together. Add the cream and vanilla; stir until mixed well.

When the dough has risen, spread the fruit evenly on top of the dough. Pour the egg mixture over the fruit. Bake at 350° for 45 minutes, or until a toothpick inserted into the custard comes out clean. Garnish with additional fruit and/or powdered sugar, if desired. Serve warm or cold.

## Butter Spreads

I love the taste of real butter, but it's difficult to spread when it comes straight out of the refrigerator. For a smooth spreadable texture, simply whip some vegetable oil, such as canola or olive oil, into either salted or unsalted butter that has been softened. The amount of oil can be increased or decreased according to your preference. The less oil you use, the longer the butter will remain semi-solid at room temperature, and the more buttery the flavor. Since it's a bit messy to clean up, I like to make a couple of batches at a time and store the excess in the freezer. The measurements below are easily multiplied or divided for the amount needed.

For each recipe, blend the ingredients in a blender or food processor until smooth, scraping down the sides of the bowl as needed. Pour the mixture into an airtight container and store in the refrigerator and/or freezer. Alternatively, add a few drops of food coloring to tint the butter, if desired, and pour into decorative candy molds. Chill until firm; remove from molds and store between sheets of waxed paper in an airtight container in the fridge or freezer.

### Basic Better Butter

2 sticks butter, softened

½ cup vegetable oil of choice

### Honey Better Butter

2 sticks butter, softened

½ cup vegetable oil of choice

2-4 tablespoons honey (to taste)

### Raspberry Better Butter

2 sticks butter, softened

½ cup vegetable oil of choice

1 cup fresh or frozen raspberries, thawed

2 tablespoon sugar

### Orange Better Butter

2 sticks butter, softened

½ cup vegetable oil of choice

2 t. fresh orange zest or grated orange peel

2 tablespoon orange juice

# Garlic & Herb Better Butter

2 sticks butter, softened

½ cup vegetable oil of choice

3 cloves minced garlic

3 tablespoon minced parsley

No More Bricks!